(61 ... or 749-5537)

The Faith of Parents

As Your Child Begins
Formal Religious Schooling

by
Maria Harris

49 Children learn to pray
when prayer is modeled
by their parents from
earliest infancy
(like acquiring a love
for reading books)

52/53 attitudes modeled
54f church community

PAULIST PRESS
New York/Mahwah, N.J.

60 ctr # for Frances (VR's care?)
J's way?

85 STORY

Library of Congress Cataloging-in-Publication Data

Harris, Maria.
    The faith of parents : as your child begins formal religious schooling / Maria Harris.
        p.   cm.
    Includes bibliographical references.
    ISBN 0-8091-3268-0 (pbk.)
    1. Parents—Religious life.   2. Parenting—Religious aspects—Catholic Church.   3. Christian education of children.
    4. Catholic Church—Education.   I. Title.
    BX2352.H37   1991
    248.8′45—dc20   91-25345
                                                              CIP

Published by Paulist Press
997 Macarthur Boulevard
Mahwah, NJ 07430

Printed and bound in the
United States of America

Contents

DEDICATION

For Michael and Lisa
Gordana and Brian
Kevin and Patty

And for Kathy

Introduction

If you are a young Catholic parent, one of life's more "teachable moments" comes when your children begin formal religious instruction—either in a parochial school program or in parish CCD. Their religious *education,* of course, has been going on all of their young lives, in both formal and informal ways. At this point, however, they are entering a new phase, one as filled with possibilities for you as for them. They may be coming home and startling you with different insights, practices, and ways of looking at your faith. ("We have an Advent wreath in school, Mom. Can we get one for here too?") They may be raising new religious questions. ("Do you think God is a woman?") They may be causing you to realize, in a sobering light, that they are touched by the way you live your life. ("Dad, I miss you. Why are you gone so much?")

As a parent facing this situation, this book is for you. It is designed to help you walk new paths with your children. But it is not *primarily* a set of suggestions for how to develop your child's faith. Instead, it is a way of deepening your own. Especially if you are one of today's many parents who have received very little formal religious schooling, this book is an opportunity to reconsider your personal religious identity. In some areas, it may even lead you to renew your religious convictions.

The Faith of Parents is written so you can use it easily, either alone or with other parents who have similar concerns. You can read it through, chapter by chapter, or move around in it as you wish. You will see that it is organized around three themes: remembering, roles and resources—remembering, in order to make connections between your own childhood experiences and those of your children; roles, in order to think about the different ways you relate with your children; resources, in order to make it clear you need not go it alone. May you find *The Faith of Parents* a source of wisdom and strength. May it assist you in your own religious call to parenting. May it guide you in nourishing the faith of the children you love so much.

Maria Harris

Part One: Remembering

The faith of parents can be understood through the religious activity of *remembering*. We do one form of remembering in our *minds,* recalling experiences from the past, and reliving them in our thoughts. But a second kind of remembering is *religious:* remembering as bringing back into the present something or someone who is apparently past; making the memory live again in the present. Actually, as Catholics, we do this second kind of remembering whenever we celebrate eucharist: we remember Jesus, and his blessing of bread and wine, and the giving of his body and blood not only as something from the past; we remember it as action going on today.

These first four chapters ask us to engage in both forms of remembering: mental and spiritual. First, we will be asked to remember our experience of church, second, to recollect our religious education; third, to recall our images of God, and, finally, to remember our experience of childhood.

Each chapter has three parts, beginning with a brief quieting time, an opportunity to center ourselves in the present where we can raise questions about the relation of our own remembering to the lives of our children. Second is a set of comments on the chapter's particular theme: church, religious education, God, childhood. The third part of each chapter is made up of suggestions of practical ways we can engage in further exploration of how our faith, as parents, can be a kind of sacrament, bringing grace to our own children.

1

Remembering Church

[A Beginning Pause: Taking a Few Moments To Become Quiet.

As you begin this first reflection, take a few moments to become still. Sit comfortably and quietly, with your eyes closed, and let go of whatever cares and concerns are distracting you at the moment. Allow yourself to release them, even if that is only for a short while. Take the phone off the hook if you need to; this is time for you to be in touch with your own faith. Now, give yourself the leisure to respond to the following questions, taking as long as you need with each:

What does the word "church" mean to you?

When you were the age your children are now, did "church" have the same meaning it has for you today? Where and how are the meanings different? Where and how are the meanings the same?

What about *pictures* and *images* of church? What were they then? What are they now? Are there differences?

Do you remember the changes that happened in the church after Vatican II? Do you remember any of your own reactions to those changes?

Do you remember your parents' reactions to the changes of Vatican II (and whether your mother's was different from your father's)—whether they were happy or disturbed by them? What about your parents' reactions today, after the last twenty-five or thirty years?

If you had to name some ways the church has been important in your life (if it has), what would those be? If you can't name any, can you say why not?

Are there any people who demonstrate a good meaning of "church" for you by the way they live? If so, can you say why?

Do you think of *yourself* as demonstrating a meaning of church?]

Father Matt is a well-loved priest who spends several hours each week with the first grade religion class. One day he was talking to the children about different ways creation pleases God. He was telling them that trees make God happy by being trees; that cats make God happy by being cats; that clams make God happy by being the best clams they can be. Then he led up to his big question. He asked the kids how they thought that boys and girls, and grownups too, could make God happy. The six year olds thought about that very seriously. Finally Jennie jumped up, almost singing the words: "I know, Father Matt. I know!"

"How, Jennie?"

"We make God happy by being as people-ly as possible," she grinned.

And everybody clapped.

"As-people-ly as possible." Not a bad way of talking about, thinking about, the meaning of church that has developed since the Second Vatican Council. That's because the past thirty years or so have been witness to an enormous change in the Catholic understanding of church. And the core of the change has been that today Catholic teaching focuses on the church as "people of God."

People of God. Giving glory to God by being people. Even being "as-people-ly as possible." That's an ancient biblical understanding, but somehow for several centuries in the life of the church, it was not a highlight. Instead, most adult Catholics who grew up in the earlier part of this century, and in the century before, learned as children a definition of church that went something like this: "The church is the congregation of all those who profess the faith of Christ, partake of the same sacraments, and are governed by their lawful pastors under one visible head, the pope." That wasn't wrong, of course, but it did make for a different emphasis! Ask your parents, ask your grandparents, if they remember that definition. They probably will.

But you probably won't. And that gives you an idea of how important it is to examine your own understanding of church, because no living generation has been as affected by changes in the image of church as those younger adults who are now parents of children beginning formal religious instruction. As members of this generation, you have lived through vast changes during your own growing-up years. You have probably been touched by these changes. And you may also be aware that everyone has an opinion about which changes have been good, and which haven't!

But there is general agreement on the major reason for the changes: the Vatican Council (Vatican II), of all the world's bishops, that met from 1961 to 1965. At that

7

meeting, over the four year period, a document was published, called "The Constitution on the Church"—a document that helped produce revolution and transformation *through an image*. And the image was—and is—of the church as "people of God" or, more simply, *church as people*. Since that revolutionary document, a literal change of consciousness has come about in Catholic self-understanding. And although the change is by no means complete, we are able to name some of its features and find out some of its implications for the faith of today's parents.

A *first* feature of the image of church as people of God is that our humanness and our bodiliness are important. People are not pure spirits: we are flesh and blood, and capable of both pleasure and pain. We are heirs to both the heights and the depths of everything human. When God became human in the person of Jesus of Nazareth, God took this humanity with utmost seriousness. Now it is our turn to take our humanity with a similar seriousness, even to the point where we acknowledge that God is still becoming human, this time in every one of us.

This is a *second* feature of the church as people of God: The Word is continually becoming flesh, in us and in our children. For not only are we a people; we are a people with a God-directed vocation. We are remembering another ancient teaching: there is a *universal* call to be God's people, a universal call to holiness. "Vocation" is no longer a word exclusive to priests, nuns and brothers, and "holy" doesn't mean stuffy or dull. Instead, as people of God, as church-in-the-world, our lives are to be lived in response to the call to be holy, to be God's people, wherever we are. We do not need to leave our daily lives and join monasteries or convents. Instead, because of our baptism into the church, our vocation is to be a people of God where we find ourselves. We are expected to bloom where we are planted.

This helps us to discover a *third* feature: we are called to be church in our homes and our places of work, and not only in the *place* or the *building* called "church." As parents, this means we are called to be church in the midst of our families, with our husbands, our wives— with other adults when we are raising our children alone—and in the daily loving, feeding, playing with, laughing and crying that make up our lives together. For the central meaning of church is not a building, or a place. The central meaning of church is a community of *people* called by the gospel to make God present in the world.

A community of people called by the gospel to be a presence of God in the world. No one can live this vocation alone. And so our strength and devotion to the vocation of our lives is (ideally) reinforced and nourished by meeting others in some form of local community, some community outside the small "domestic church"—little micro-church—comprised of our family. This wider local community is the parish, often but not always a neighborhood unit made up of others like us: fighting the same battles, knowing the same sorrows, dreaming the same dreams.

But the parish is also made up of people *not* like us: old people living alone, people of other races, recent immigrants, people living in residences for the terminally ill or with crippling disabilities, all of whom remind us of worlds outside our own family, ways of living different from ours. Together we form a mosaic, a multi-colored splendor. Together we draw nourishment from the sacraments, from acting for justice, from visiting the sick, from one another. The parish is the place where we "gather the folk, break the bread, tell the story, and go forth to live the gospel."

As our children begin a more direct relation to this local community, through the catechesis and teaching that involves them in sacramental life (especially eucharist, penance and confirmation, but their baptisms too), our own relation with the community is generally in for some change. At the least we will be attending meetings with other parents like us, and at most we may be hosting meetings or acting as catechists in our own homes.

And so we need to be ready for a crisis—crisis not in the sense of a dreadful ordeal, but crisis in the sense of a special time: a time of new patterns, new possibilities and new ways of living. Crisis in the sense of an invitation to take on a mature, adult religious faith: the faith of parents.

Our children's new involvement will be the source of this crisis, and we will probably find ourselves responding to their increased awareness by an awakening of our own. Most of us will find our adult faith affected by greater fidelity and attention to doing what we do and being who we are: we will have neither the time nor the reason to add activities to our days. Others of us will shift our involvements so we will be able to take on opportunities—through the parish—to probe our religious lives more carefully: through retreats, or going back to school, or volunteering in outreach or hunger projects.

Still others of us may take on roles within the church: as lectors, food pantry directors, RCIA sponsors, especially if our local parish is without a resident priest.

But whatever our response, we need to be alert to the truth that by being parents, we have been brought into a time and place where the question of ourselves as church is bound to be raised. If we respond to that question, and become more self-conscious of ourselves as church-in-the-world, we will be continuing and completing the work of Vatican II. We will be re-creating and reshaping the church of the future for ourselves and our children. Before the face of God, we will be becoming "as people-ly as possible."

FOR FURTHER EXPLORATION

1. *The Church in Poetry: Families Creating Cinquains:* Cinquains (short, five-line poems) can be used in many ways: as conversation starters, as play, as ways to explore a particular understanding. Here we use them to find out some of the meanings of church in our family (we can do this same exercise in adult groups). The directions are:

   Line 1: Give a one-word name, subject of the poem. In this case it is "church."
   Line 2: Give two words to describe the first line.
   Line 3: Follow this with three action words.
   Line 4: Create a phrase descriptive of the subject.
   Line 5: Summarize in one word.

Example: Church.
Peoples moving.
Meeting, loving, blessing.
Always there for us.
Home.

2. *Interviewing Grandparents (or Older Members of Our Local Parish).* This is an interview conducted, ideally, by parent and child together. If grandparents are not available or, for example, live out of town, ask your pastoral staff for names of three to five people over seventy who belong to your parish. Then ask if they would be willing to be interviewed on their memory of church as it has changed throughout their lifetimes. The same questions that appear in the opening reflection section of this chapter can be used.

3. *A Reading Group for Parents.* To follow up and to deepen your own understanding of church, begin a reading group where you meet to discuss books on recent developments in the church, or read some of the following on your own.

Abbott, Walter M., S. J. (ed.) *The Documents of Vatican II.* New York: Guild Press, 1966. "Constitution on the Church."

Bausch, William J. *The Hands-On Parish.* Mystic: Twenty-Third Publications, 1989.

Boff, Leonardo. *Ecclesiogenesis. The Base Communities Reinvent the Church.* Maryknoll: Orbis Books, 1986.

Dulles, Avery. *Models of the Church.* New York: Doubleday and Co., 1974.

Harris, Maria. *Fashion Me a People*. Louisville: Westminster/John Knox, 1989.

Kennedy, Eugene. *Tomorrow's Catholics, Yesterday's Church*. New York: Harper and Row, 1988.

Leckey, Dolores R. *Laity Stirring the Church*. Philadelphia: Fortress Press, 1987.

Ruether, Rosemary Radford. *Women-Church. Theology and Practice of Feminist Liturgical Communities*. San Francisco: Harper and Row, 1985.

2

Remembering Religious Education

[*A Beginning Pause: Taking a Few Moments To Become Quiet.*

Take off your shoes; loosen your tie. Sit back in your soul—the way to do that is to sit back in your body. This pause is a time to get in touch with your own experience and memory of your early religious education, when you were the age of your own children—and before, as well as, perhaps, after. To make the most of this reflection, allow yourself to become still, inside and out. Allow yourself to feel centered. Tell your children that for the next few moments you will be taking some quiet, quality time, and ask them if they want to join you. If they do, remind them they will need to be quiet too.

What are some of the things you know—really *know* in your flesh and in your bones? (For example, that God is good; that life includes suffering; that dawn always follows night; that we can depend on some people for anything—or perhaps something more uniquely personal.)

How do you know what you know? How early do you remember learning it?

Have you any basic beliefs and understandings

(about life, love, perhaps God and religion) you are quite sure you got from your own parents?

Have you any basic beliefs and understandings you realize differ from those of your parents?

Can you name the two or three most important "teachers" of your childhood (not necessarily school-teachers though it is all right to include them)? Can you recall what it was they taught you?

Can you name the two or three most important *stories* from your childhood, stories that have been guides during your life?

Can you name the most important truths, or beliefs, or convictions you would like your children to learn in their lives? And can you say why?]

Although this book is for parents whose children are beginning their formal religious *schooling,* it would be a mistake to think that your children are only now beginning their formal religious *education*. The difference is that religious education begins at least at birth (and probably long before in the past generations who have made us who we are), while schooling begins when children begin to think and study in more structured ways, including using books. Your child is not going off to religion classes "cold." Instead she or he is beginning these classes with the wealth of religious education you and others have given during the first five, six or seven years of life.

Parents as Primary Educators

No way exists to avoid the awesome truth that parents are their children's major religious educators, though you don't educate by being instructors as much as by being parents. This was brought home to me recently as I watched a videotape of Christopher, who has now reached the ripe old age of one! His parents—lucky enough to have a portable camera—received him into life by recording the high points of his first year: his birth, his first Christmas, his christening, his welcome into his family and into his church. If you have videotapes that are similar, you might want to make some comparisons.

The video of infant Christopher is a perfect example of how religious education begins, and then continues, in everything parents do, although it tends to have two major forms. First, religious education is *physical;* second, it is *storied*.

Physical Religious Education

Like some of your own first films or recordings, Christopher's video begins in the hospital, a few hours after his birth. The education going on is entirely *physical,* like all religious education during the first year or two of life. If you watch his mom and dad with him, you can see by the way they hold him that they believe he is precious and beyond price, just as someone watching you with your baby learns a great deal. It's also clear Christopher's parents experience birth and their newborn son as some kind of miracle: they haven't yet gotten used to them.

Although Christopher obviously doesn't understand words, the tone his parents use in talking to him shows their attitude to him: "Oh, what a wonderful boy you are!" "Such a perfect smile!" "Just look at the marvelous shape of your hands." Over and over, he is told how loved he is, how welcome. And although he doesn't receive their words into his mental memory, he receives their touch and their gentleness and care as they hold him into his biological memory, into his *physical* self. Those first days after his birth are the beginning of his religious education: the experiences of warmth, security, trust and love on which his later religious *schooling* will build.

This *physical* education, when a child is "simply religious" through and through, is a child's learning whatever is to be learned through its body. On the parents' part, the physical education happens through holding, caressing, speaking, bathing, changing; it happens through feeding and clothing; it happens during the night when the infant's cries are heard and responded to. It happens as parents provide "zones of quiet": protection from too much stimulation in the way of sight, and from too much or too intense sound.

On the baby's part, the physical education goes on not only through its receptivity to its parents' actions, but also through its *own* looking, touching and handling— first of its own body, and then of objects beyond—based on desires to look, touch and handle that are as urgent for a child as hunger, and as necessary for education as books will be later on. This physical education is equally powerful as a child learns to turn over, to crawl, to stand and finally to achieve that always-to-be-marveled at miracle: to walk.

Religiously, the educational meaning of all this is enormous for so-called "normal" children, but in some ways even more for children who are disabled in some way. Everything said physically can be a statement about

17

creation, incarnation, promise and hope. Every com-
forting touch is a statement about love. Every concrete
meeting with someone or something in creation lays the
ground for living a sacramental life later on. For sacramental life is based on the belief that all created reality,
but especially bread, food, oil and water, loving and
reverent human touch, and the gesture of forgiveness
can be an avenue along which God enters human life.

The first catechesis and schooling will be *talk* about
these realities, important talk; the first religious education is the *experience* of them.

Storied Religious Education

The second great form of religious education during the early childhood years is best named the "mythical" or "storied" form (though like the physical, it is a
form that continues throughout life). This is the form
that develops as a child begins to speak, from the first
magical word (often "mama") that indicates—given
most adults' delighted response—the child's powers to
influence the universe, to the capacity to put words together in sentences, and eventually to make those words
into stories.

As these powers develop, and as the hearing and
understanding of words becomes stronger, a child, listening to stories—of family, nation and religion, or of
mythical people such as the characters in folk tales or
fairy-tales—begins to realize that life has a shape to it, a
form to it. Life has beginnings, endings, freedom, fail-
ure, hope. Later on a child will learn that in religion
these are named Genesis, crucifixion, exodus, sin, and
resurrection.

18

In learning and listening to stories, meeting with dragons and witches, wise and wily animals, royal princesses and heroes, and then re-creating and retelling the tales, children come to grips with forces in the universe (like good and evil, terror and celebration, life and death) that, until the power of story/myth became theirs, had no names. But once they can be named, they can also be faced. Like *physical* forms, *storied* forms are in the fabric of genuine religious education.

Weaving the Fabric of Religious Education

When formal schooling begins, as is now happening with your child, these *physical* and *storied* forms of religious education are not left behind. Instead, schooling becomes interwoven with them as an additional, great thread in a tapestry already well begun.

The first great weaver of these threads of *the physical, the storied* and *schooling,* is the God of all creation.

The second is the child who is co-weaver with God.

But the weaving will not happen as it might unless other weavers are present: the significant and caring adults who provide the physical and storied beginnings, and continue to offer them throughout life. These adults are a child's parents.

Attempting this weaving as parents, we will make many mistakes, as all parents do, and when that happens we will have the good sense to ask for help. We will have many successes, as all parents do, and when they happen we will marvel things turned out so beautifully. We will become attuned to those children in our world who are without weavers in their lives, and seek to remedy that. Out of such experiences we will offer many prayers and probably light many candles, realizing the task of parenting is too much for mere mortals without divine assistance. But if our hearts are attuned to the continuing miracle our child is always being and becoming, we will not fail in the end. Instead we will provide a grounded experience of life, love and education strong enough to last our children till the time when they become parents themselves.

FOR FURTHER EXPLORATION

1. If you do not already do so, design with your children a ritual of grace before and after meals. Be sure it has several physical components (for example, joining hands in a particular way, bowing the head, keeping a brief silence, holding up the food for a blessing, lighting a candle, humming a tune, etc.) and several storied components (ritual phrases such as "Let us remember those without food in our city," or "Let us remember the day we had ice cream," or "Let us treat the bread before us as Jesus treated the bread of Passover," etc.).

2. If you do not already do so, engage in the practice of telling a Bible story before bedtime (for example, about some of the animals in the ark, about Noah, about the good shepherd, about the woman with the lost coin). Take care not to frighten children with stories of wolves or hirelings while they are too young to understand these.

   But intersperse these mythical tales with those from the treasury of fairy tales, too: from Hans Christian Andersen and the Brothers Grimm or from more modern sources such as *Sesame Street* and *Free To Be You and Me*.

3. For Mothers *and* Fathers: If you do not already do so, at least once a month engage in the activity of baking bread with your child (even if it is from a mix). Make at least one loaf for yourselves, to receive a special blessing designed as in #1, and at least one to be given to the hungry or the homeless of your city.

3

Remembering God

[*A Beginning Pause: Taking a Few Moments To Become Quiet.*

Take the phone off the hook, and sit quietly in your favorite place. Tell the kids this is Mommy and/or Daddy's *place* to be with God, and their *time* to be quiet. Ask them either to be quiet with you, or to give you this quiet time as a present for the next few minutes. Then close your eyes and let your body relax gently. Don't hurry. Instead, let the responses emerge at their own pace. When you're ready, take as long as you need to reflect on the following questions.

As you think back to yourself at the age your children are now, do you remember what you thought about God: who God was, or where, or what God was like?

Do you remember what you thought about God's relation to yourself—whether God cared about you in any special ways?

What were some of the feelings you had about God?

Did you pray regularly? If you did, was that at particular times of the day or night?

Did you have spontaneous conversations with God? Or were your contacts with God more set and formal—through prayers like the "Our Father" or ceremonies like mass?

Was your childhood experience of God ever scary? Was it a source of comfort and delight? Or was it sometimes a combination of both?

With your own children, is there anything you would like to repeat of your images and experience of God? Is there anything you would like to avoid?]

Sometimes we hear that when children are small, they do not think their parents are like God; instead, they think that God is like their parents. That may be true for some children, but as adults, remembering back to our childhood understandings of God, we are often aware that we had the wisdom, no matter how young we were, to sense the reality called "God" was in many ways the "more than" of everyone or everything: more than our parents in knowing things, more than the ocean in beauty, more than a Christmas of gifts in delight.

As adults, some of us can describe such memories clearly:

> As a small child one of my favorite festivals was Trinity Sunday. It seemed to me quiet and beautiful, and happening around midsummer became associated in my mind with green trees and flowers in bloom. It was "mysterious" and right, something far bigger than the words used in church about it which sounded to a small child nonsense. But Trinity wasn't nonsense, it was Holy, Holy, Holy as we sang in the hymn, and even a very young child could join in a sort of "oneness" with all things bright and beautiful and worship this Something so great and lovely that it didn't matter at all that it was not understood. It just Was.

so sweet

so great

Others of us remember because of our parents' or grandparents' attitudes. A twenty-three year old woman, when asked about her memories, said, "Neither my mother nor father attempted to explain or describe God to me. God was indescribable as far as I was concerned, a creator. But I am sure my parents increased my sense of God's . . . mystery by their own awe and reserve in discussing the subject." And Helen Flexner, a Quaker, talks about the impact of her grandfather's quiet time on her own life:

> As a child I was told that grandfather spent an hour every morning and evening listening to God. So when I came suddenly upon my grandfather one day seated motionless in his armchair with closed eyes, I knew he was not asleep. He was talking with God. I stopped short where I was and stood very still. Perhaps if I listened intently enough, I might hear God's voice speaking to my grandfather. But the room remained quiet; not even the faintest whisper reached my ears. After a long time my grandfather opened his eyes, saw me and smiled at me gently. These moments of intense listening for God's voice in the room with my grandfather are among the most vivid memories of my early childhood.

We, too, probably have our memories of God. For some of us, God was the one who listened to our secrets—the one we spoke to easily and naturally at the close of the day as we tried to say our prayers with sleep closing over us.

For others of us, God was Father: tender and caring, source of all things, the one whose name was "hallowed" (although as we got older, some joker taught us the line "Harold be thy name").

Others of us always approached God through the Blessed Virgin Mary, and although we never called Our Blessed Mother "God," our intuition probably was that Mary represented God's maternal face.

Still others of us had an early sense that God was on the side of the poor—maybe because we were poor too—and that when we heard the name "God" we were hearing about someone who could be relied on to wipe our tears away.

And to be honest, many—perhaps too many—of us were scared, frightened of God, imagining God as a strict and punishing judge, out to get us.

Finally, others of us who are today's parents had no contact with God. We grew up in circumstances where the question of God—absent *or* present—was not one of life's questions.

Now, however, the God question is with us in new and very personal ways, and it's important to take some time with it not only for ourselves, but for our children. This new phase of their religious education will be raising the meaning of God, if it hasn't happened already, not only for them, but for us. So it is important to ask the questions: How *might* we think about God? Do we have any clues from the church, from the world?

In our time it helps to know that the question of God is being given a new prominence. *First,* attention to language about men and women (so-called "sexist" language) has raised the issue of ways to speak of God, so that God is not always he, or always she, or even he *and* she. The Maguires' son Tommy says God is "a man, a lady and a kid"—another form of Trinity. When asked why, he says, "Because the kid god makes kids." In the gospel according to Tommy, as his father puts it, how else could kids be in God's image, God's likeness?

Attending to language has made many aware that on the one hand God is *beyond* every image, including he and she. But on the other hand, because of the way our minds work, we human beings need to use our imaginations in approaching God. Actually, there are many, many ways to speak of God: shepherd, king, messiah, yes—but also mother, bakerwoman, housekeeper, brooding hen sheltering her chicks. Kid. And rock, fire, breath and beauty too.

A *second* influence on God-understandings today comes from conversation among peoples of different religions and ethnic groups. Where many of us grew up in neighborhoods or schools or settings where one religion or race or nationality prevailed, the global character of our living today—and the all-pervasive influence of television—has made us aware God is not a Christian (as distinct from a Jew, a Muslim, a Buddhist); God is not white; God is not Irish, or Italian or Polish. Instead, the God who is God is the God of all peoples (each of whom, like us, is a "people of God") and named by some of them as Yahweh, by others as Allah, by others as G-d, by others as the Great Spirit, and by still others as the One beyond all names. In addition, that God is often *not* omnipotent or all knowing: instead, God is a suffering God who changes even as we do.

Third, the rediscovery of the biblical God by all Christians, but especially by Catholic Christians in basic Christian communities of Latin America and Africa, is a rediscovery reminding the whole church that the God revealed most prominently in the Bible is the God of the

26

poor, the God of the downtrodden, the God of the forgotten. God is on the side of those most in need. This is the God Jesus preached, out of his own Jewish tradition:

> The Spirit of the Lord is upon me,
> because he has chosen me to preach the good news to
> the poor.
> He has sent me to proclaim liberty to the captives,
> and recovery of sight to the blind;
> to set free the oppressed (Lk 4:18).

In the face of such influences, what might parents do, as we explore our own experiences and memories of God? That will depend not only on us personally, on our children, and on our relations with them, but on our relations with their teachers and catechists, and on the parish we belong to, as well as on the wider society where we live our lives.

Still, certain rules can help us as we try to assist our children in their coming to be with God.

1. Names and meanings of God need to be *appropriate,* appropriate *to* God, and able to be appropriated *by* us and our children. The point here is that we need to remember to speak with some tentativeness about God because *no* words really "say" God. But with this attitude conveyed, we can then proceed to share those names most cherished in our faith: God as Father as well as Mother, God as creator, even creative artist, God as Spirit, and God as love, where those who abide in love abide in God, and God in them.

2. We also need ways to understand God that are social and prophetic. Parents can contribute to a worldview that is basically in error if we concentrate on a per-

27

sonal and private God without broader connections. Doing that can eliminate God's relation to society, to the mystical body of Christ that includes all of the world's peoples as well as the body of the world itself. For the Christian's God is one who is involved in re-creating the world to be a place of hope, healing and promise for everyone. As a song sung in many Sunday liturgies reminds us: "The Lord hears the cry of the poor; blessed be the Lord."

3. We need to give our children the sense of a God who is *attainable*. The religious word here is *immanent*—a word that means God is not only *within* all reality, but that God is *the* within of all reality: the wateriness of water; the starlight of starlight; the love of love. Understanding God as attainable suggests that no place is God's special place because every place is one where a child might meet God. No time is God's special moment, because every moment is a possibility for finding God. And each person is God's special person because every person is in the image of God.

Remembering these rules for our own lives is critical if we are to convey them to our children. Remembering these understandings *into* our children's lives is our vocation and our responsibility as parents.

FOR FURTHER EXPLORATION

1. Play the game, "God is . . ." with your children. Begin with a short prayer, where together you remember that God is with you now. Then each one has three turns, where she or he fills in a word or an image that completes the phrase, "God is . . ." After that, take

time to talk about what you heard from one another, which answer touched you most, what you think it might mean.

When you have finished, do the same with "God is not . . ." If you play this game seriously (though not solemnly) and with reverence, it can make God more real and perhaps reveal some surprising faces of God to each of you.

2. Take a sheet of paper and draw an image of yourself, an image of your child, and an image of God. It need not be a drawing of something concrete; it can be an abstract symbol, or a drawing of something that is representative: a rock, a tree, a river, a garden.

Next, on a piece of paper, imagine God as male. List ten qualities of God that occur to you. Then, imagining God as female, do the same thing.

Finally, redraw your original images. When you reimagine the divinity, has making the lists influenced your images of yourself, your child, your God differently? If so, in what ways? What new discoveries do you make? Do you have any resistances?

3. In this chapter, we read Jesus' echoing the words of the prophet Isaiah speaking of God's care for the poor. Reread these biblical words as they might be in interplay with your images of God, experiences of God, and your prayer at this present time.

Remembering Childhood

[*A Beginning Pause: Taking a Few Moments To Become Quiet.*

In this chapter we're going to do some of the work of recalling our childhood, and bringing our memory of it into conversation with the adults we are today.

Start by taking a few moments to become still. Begin with some deep breathing: eight or ten long breaths, with a pause after each. When you notice a growing stillness, sit back in your soul by sitting back in your body. Close your eyes and allow the *feeling* of being centered to flow through your body. When you're ready, open your eyes and take some time with each of the following questions.

At what age do the memories of your childhood begin?

When you do start remembering, do you have any one overriding feeling: of security, or love, or happiness, or of loneliness and something approaching pain? Or is the memory a mixture: of pleasure *and* pain, of delight *and* disappointment, of mystery *and* revelation?

Is there any outstanding memory of the first six or seven years that you recall? If so, what is it, and why do you think it is outstanding for you?

Do you feel tenderness or nostalgia for the child you *were*? If so, can you sit with the memory of that for a while, and perhaps let it wash over you?

Do you remember the feeling of *time* in your childhood? Was time long and leisurely—different in feeling from the way it is for you now?

Do you remember the feeling of *place* in your childhood? Are there places you can return to immediately? If so, what are they like?

Is there a particular place you always think of as "home"?]

Childhood—our own as well as that of our children—can never be fully understood. One reason is that our earliest years are generally not accessible to us, or remembered only in fragments. Another is that certain dimensions of our early experiences can only be grasped later on in life, when we have the adult ability to make connections not possible earlier, simply because we hadn't lived long enough. Still another is that childhood is a mystery, not in the sense that we cannot know *anything* about it, but in the sense that we cannot know *everything* about it. And, finally, there are certain memories in childhood—perhaps especially painful ones—that do not reemerge for us in later memory until we are ready for them.

As adults we carry our childhood within us, and often, during adult life, we eventually make "sense" of our childhood, and therefore of ourselves. Similarly our children carry *their* childhood too, a childhood uniquely theirs. In our culture a great temptation for adults is to hurry that childhood, or to fill it with preparation for adolescence and adulthood, even for college, university and business. The memory of our own childhood could serve as a brake on this too-quick direction toward the future, and teach us that a central gift of childhood, pertinent to their being educated religiously, is time—more specifically, childhood time.

Understanding the special quality of childhood time sometimes comes to us late. I remember when it finally took hold of me as an adult. I was teaching the third grade, and loved teaching religion. Without realizing it, I discovered that as each new class came in to my room, I was saying to myself, at least subconsciously, "These children will be with me until June. I have this year to teach them the whole of Christianity, everything about God and Jesus and Mary; everything about baptism and holy communion." And then a wonderful thing happened. I got promoted to the fourth grade! (And began saying, "I have this entire year . . .") Eventually I had the good sense to realize there would never be a year when a child—or an adult—would "get it all." Instead, living a life, being a person, going to God—all of these *were* the work of a lifetime. You *never* needed to "get it all," because life was for that. And time was the atmosphere where this would happen. Time: God's good time. Time: Childhood time.

Time has a different feel to a child. If you are thirty now, a year is a small fraction of your life—one thirtieth, to be exact. But if you are five, time is forever, and a year is twenty percent of your entire life!

"When I was a little kid," says twelve year old Tim, "about six years old, I used to think it would be forever till I was twelve."

"Well, that really wasn't such a long time ago, was it?" responds his mother.

32

"Not a long time! Not a long time!" he repeats. "Mom, it's been half my life!"

The sense and the feel of time in childhood is leisurely. This rich, full feeling of time ought to be cultivated, so that a child deepens the experience begun in the storied stage; the experience of knowing life has a form and a shape. Adults, parents and teachers, will actually have to teach a few things to children: do no harm to any living creature or to the earth; receive each day as a gift; look both ways before you cross the street. But on the whole, the first years of life and even later childhood ought to be governed by the principle: Just let the kids grow up. Give them time—childhood time.

For at its roots, childhood is not designed for the accumulation of facts (although around eight or nine things like ballplayers' averages and the names of the capitals of the fifty states do seem to enter the system naturally). Instead, childhood is basically the time for getting a sense of what it is to be a person, what it is to be human. Childhood is the time for coming to understand what it is to belong to a people. Childhood is the time for learning what it is to live on planet earth. And parents' tasks include drawing on our own adult faith to do this by providing three experiences: presence, receptivity and responsibility.

1. *Presence.* To know themselves, and to be in community with other people, children need to have the sense they are subjects, originators, creators. They are not objects, property to be used. But they will not have this sense of themselves as subjects unless other people mirror that back to them. It is not enough for them to see themselves; they must see other people seeing them—appreciating, valuing and cherishing them.

33

All of us realize that the sense of ourselves as being in a human community doesn't exist simply because someone stands next to us physically—we've all had the experience of feeling alone in a crowd. But when someone is *humanly* present to us, we know it, no matter how young we are. They take us seriously. They see us, they hear us, they are at our disposal.

The family is the primary place where adults offer this presence to children, and where the child begins to understand herself or himself as a person and as a "subject." They do this in the Washington family with the three kids: Keesha, eight, Darryl, six, and Ty, four. They do it with family meetings where everyone speaks and gets listened to, especially Ty; by special outings with Keesha or Darryl or Ty (usually alone) on their birthdays; by celebrating holidays together, where they stop to enjoy one another; by everyone taking turns leading grace at meals at least once a week.

2. *Receptivity.* Receptivity is the other side of presence. For children, receptivity usually takes the form of hospitality: someone lets them know they are welcome. Every kid on every block in the country can probably tell you those places where they're welcome and where they're not: who "lets them in" and who doesn't. Often the richest memories of childhood are of those people and those places where we felt received, felt not only that there was time for us, but that we also had a *place*.

In her memoir of growing up in Stamps, Arkansas, Maya Angelou tells a story of such receptivity. As a little girl, the child Maya had been raped. Soon after, the man who raped her was killed. Believing it was her words and her voice that caused his death, and fearful her speech could do further harm, the child stopped speaking. But Mrs. Bertha Flowers, the aristocrat of black Stamps, and a neighbor to Maya's grandmother, didn't ask the child to speak. She did, however, invite her into her home to have cookies and lemonade, and honored her silence while she was there.

One of the first times Maya visited, the older woman took down *A Tale of Two Cities* from the bookcase. "It was the best of times and the worst of times . . ." she read, in a voice full of grace and gravity. Angelou says that listening to that voice was like listening to singing. It made her feel she had a place. Eventually, warmed by the hospitality and receptivity of subsequent visits, the child regained her voice.

3. *Responsibility* follows from presence and receptivity. Once children learn to live in time and to live in place—that is, once they learn *presence* and *receptivity*—they discover the human vocation is to respond. As children begin to do this responding, guided by their parents from infancy onward, they are actually developing the moral side of life: to be in a *responsible* relation to everyone and everything.

Educating this capacity for responsibility, this power to be moral, is often limited to our giving "do's" and "don'ts" to children. Or we think moral education is the work of formal religious schooling or catechesis. But educating in, and into, responsibility arises primarily from the faith of parents, and in the setting of the family, as each new person and each new thing a child meets calls forth from the child some kind of answer, some kind of response. "There was a child went forth every day," wrote Walt Whitman, "And the first object he look'd upon, that object he became,/ And that object became part of him for the day or a certain part of the day,/ Or for many years or stretching cycles of years."

To help make responsibility real in a child's life, parents' work is particular and practical. It involves helping the child see the difference between being responsible *to* and being responsible *for*. Often children are confused by this: thinking they are responsible *for* everything and everyone (such as their parents' relation with each other, or a divorce, or even a death), while believing they are responsible *to* very few.

Actually the opposite is true. As human beings we are responsible *for* ourselves and our actions from earliest childhood—although in the beginning we need help in learning to realize this—while we are responsible *to* all creation. Such learning can be fostered in the family when children are given opportunities, through care for pets and plants and pots and pans, to grow toward greater responsibility *for* themselves in the great journey through life, while learning from those who take their childhood time seriously that the moral vocation is to be responsible *to* all things and *to* all people. To learn this in childhood is to be ready for the rest of life.

FOR FURTHER EXPLORATION

1. Walt Whitman is quoted in this chapter. Go back and memorize this brief set of lines. Then explore how these words describe your child's life. What is she or he meeting each day? What is becoming part of her or him? What do you want to encourage? What do you want to discourage?

2. By yourself, or with your spouse, write out or draw five things and five people *you* are responsible *to* and five things and five people you are responsible *for*.

3. With your children, write out or draw five things and five people she or he is responsible *to,* and five things and five people she or he is responsible *for*.

Part Two: Roles

When any of us take the time to think about who we are, we inevitably make new discoveries. For not only are we persons with unique and individual identities: born into this family, at this time, in this place, with this history. We are also persons who are asked to play many roles, while still remaining ourselves. To the people next door, we are "neighbors"; to our own parents, we are "son" or "daughter" or still "child"; to the people we work with we are "boss" or "driver" or "nurse." And to those who don't know us, we are even, sometimes, "Hey you!"

Many of our roles come with birth: son or daughter, for example; member of the Smith or Fisher or Spinelli family; U.S. citizen; Catholic. But other roles come later in life, and these are the ones we look at in the next four chapters. In what follows we will be spending time exploring four roles that link us intimately with our children: the role of parent; the role of model; the role of woman or man; the role of adult. Playing these roles is not "pretend" play; rather it is the serious play of our deep and powerful vocation toward the next generation.

And so we enter the consideration of these roles as we did in the Remembering section: with an attitude of stillness, of meditation, of prayer. We take time to reflect upon and to examine these roles. And finally we look at some ways we might explore them more deeply—with our loved ones or alone—in order to be even better parents, better role models, better adult men and women than we have been before.

5

The Role of Parent

[*A Beginning Pause: Taking a Few Moments To Become Quiet.*

Before you read the next several pages, prepare yourself by becoming quiet. Find the place in the house that you consider most comfortable; sit down with your spouse or your children—or alone if that feels better—and let your tiredness go. Untense any muscles that seem too tight; breathe deeply and regularly. You are searching for the still point within yourself, the center that has the capacity to be calm, even if everything around you seems to be on the verge of falling apart. Go with that searching and that centering, and then let the next several minutes be a reflection on your responses to the following questions:

When did the realization dawn on you that you were a parent?

Did the realization come all at once, or did it develop slowly over time?

What are the strongest positive feelings you have about your role as parent? What are the strongest negative ones?

If you are a father, what if anything is different in your role from being a mother? If you are a mother, what do you find different from the father role?

If you are raising your child or children alone, what stands out as the most important thing you want to be able to do and be for them? Where do you go for help with those wishes?

What do you want to avoid as a parent?

Are there any ways in which you are repeating things your parents did with you, in your childhood, as you attempt to parent your own children? Are there patterns you are trying to avoid?

What for you is the best thing, so far, about being a parent?]

One of my closest friends describes her experience three days after the birth of her first child, when it was time to leave the hospital. "They put the baby in my arms," she says, "and wave goodbye. None of them even *offers* to come with me. And all I want to do is shout: No, No, No: I'm not ready for this!"

Another friend nods in agreement. "I know exactly what you mean. My most vivid memory is of my husband saying goodbye to us, on his way out the door, leaving me alone with the baby for the very first time. I looked at this tiny infant, and then I said to her, out loud, and with panic in my voice: "It's just you and me. Twenty-four hours a day." And then something else dawned on me, and I added, "Maybe for eighteen years!"

The shock of parenthood can catch us unawares— certainly the first time around. With the second, third and fourth children, and after that, it becomes at least familiar, although it is a role with surprises that never end. But in the beginning, no matter how old we are, or how sophisticated and successful, the sheer fact of a human being totally dependent upon us is often overwhelming. It takes time to grow into it—time and grace. It also takes wisdom to sort out the components of the role, and to give ourselves to it as the genuine religious vocation it actually is.

In these few pages I want to highlight four elements that make up the role of parent. Sara Ruddick names the first three in a fine book called *Maternal Thinking*—a book that makes the point that fathers can be "maternal" as well as mothers. The three are protection, nourishment and training, the last of which I'd rather call *guidance*. The fourth is the ground of all three, and of all other parenting activity as well: love. All of them are holy acts, religious acts, sacramental acts. When we engage in them, God dwells in us, and we dwell in God.

Protection is the first parental act. Often, especially in the early years, parents can feel life is one long series of protective acts toward their children, and their directions are one long series of "Don'ts." But protection is absolutely necessary for children: protection *from* everything from fire, flood, ice and snow to infection, illness, and abuse. Protection *of* children's gifts and rights: their unique talents whether those are singing, dancing or a sweet disposition; their entitlement before God and humanity to health and hope for the future. Protection *for* and *in favor of* children: the protection embodied in laws that would extend health care, schooling, and safety to each of them: rich ones, poor ones, black ones, white ones, those who are athletes and those who are frail in body or spirit.

All of this makes the reality of parenthood hard and conflicting. That's because every parent knows her or his child cannot be protected from everything and every-

43

one; every parent knows his or her daughter or son can be in a situation where there is nothing the parent can do. The car that speeds toward the child, out of nowhere; the back turned from the baby for only the time it takes to answer the phone, and the baby to wander. Margot Strom, a Jewish educator, tells of an evening when her six year old daughter, puzzled, inquired of visitors in her home why they had numbers on their arms. She spoke of an inner voice saying to her, "Oh no, not yet—she is too young to hear of the camps," but at the same time she knew it was not possible to shield her child from such knowledge. Evil does exist in the world; people, including children, are killed and abused in terrifying ways; hunger and homelessness are real. Any sensitive parent can appreciate the pain of those parents who cannot protect their children, can appreciate the agony it must be to put warm cloths on the belly of your child to quiet the hunger pains because there is nothing to eat.

Nourishing is the second component in parenting—nourishing and nurturing. Physical nourishment is basic: food and shelter are every child's right and every parent's responsibility, symbolized, perhaps, in the capacity placed in a mother's body to feed an infant from her own substance. But that "own substance" is not only a mother's: it is symbol for the work both parents must do in their responsibility toward children: their earning power, their "substance" in the money sense, must be at the disposal of their children and their children's needs. On this point, one of the sins crying to heaven for vengeance, about which the official church might speak more forcibly, is the reneging on such obligations on the part of one partner, usually the father, when a marriage ends.

The nourishing of the body, however, is partner to the nourishing of the *spirit* of the child—in some ways an even more delicate activity. For human spirits are nourished in an environment of freedom, and the parent who would foster the nurturance of a whole person must necessarily often do "as if she or he were not-doing," must learn on the job the delicate line between giving too much and giving too little, must learn to change the measure of these as the child develops, must learn the different needs of different children. Nourishing (and protection too) needs to go on in such a way that children have room: to find out who they are, and to discover whatever poetry and passion lies inside their hearts.

That brings us to a third component: *guidance*. The guide is one who walks alongside, who points the way, who conveys a knowledge of the territory. Guides have generally scouted out the terrain beforehand and figured out where the pitfalls might be. But guides also have a sense of where the traveler wants to go, what equipment is needed and what may be left behind. Guides take the measure of their companions: they use their listening skills with great care in order to assess just how much their companions are able to do. And when they are really good at it, they know three or four possible routes to the same destination, working hard not to teach that there is only one way of going.

None of these elements of parenting are possible, however, without one further element: *loving*. Loving, however, does not mean an absence of anger, irritation, short temper, frustration, depression, or even a good strong yell. (Any parents who tell you they never express these vis-à-vis their children either don't know what they

are talking about or are not in touch with their feelings.)
But it does mean that parents offer their children the vast
reservoir of their own spirituality and their own adulthood—fragile as these might be—and make their resources of body and mind available to their children for
the duration of the child's life. It means they never abuse
their children physically or psychically. It means they
are willing to give their lives and their fortunes so that
this new generation might live.

And that, in turn, is, if not impossible, terribly difficult without a supportive community. Just as parents'
love is core, heart and fuel for the works of protection,
nourishment and guidance, so the surrounding community of family, neighborhood, church and school can
be the source of strength to all parents in their loving
work, their loving parenting. I write here the words "can
be" the source because, sadly, the communities around
parents are not always the kind of sources they might
be—which returns us to themes in our chapters on God
and church, and the discovery in our day of the God of
the oppressed and the church that speaks a prophetic
voice.

How so? In this chapter we have reflected on parenting as a work of protecting, nourishing and guiding
children, out of love, and with the support of community. But in our day and in our society, one out of five
children lives in poverty, the number of pediatric AIDS
cases is rising rapidly, particularly in our inner cities,
and sixty percent of the households receiving food
stamps contain children, although the average amount
received has not changed since 1980. The measure of my
community's care for *all* children is how my community
cares for our least fortunate children—and their parents.

Children as a group are a voiceless, voteless minority who have a right to protection, nourishment, guidance and love. Many parents are oppressed too, especially those who are younger, or raising children alone, or members of minorities. We also have a right to the community's concern for the least fortunate of us.

To the parents whose individual circumstances allow the fostering of their children's wholeness, a gift has been given. But they, and those of us who are not parents, must join hands as a next step so that the best of parenting becomes available for all. Our parishes and our schools need the voices of men and women who know what parenting involves, to speak in advocacy for laws that make it possible. Our communities need to draw on the faith that is in us all to go out in mercy and service, so that the role of parent can be fulfilled, in dignity and with promise, by all who receive it from God.

FOR FURTHER EXPLORATION

1. Take the time to examine how protection, nourishment and guidance are going on in your family. What are five ways you—and your children—are aware of each? What are five additional ways each might be put in place for you?

2. Design a series of parish meetings to determine which parents in your midst are most in need of help with parenting. Instead of one large meeting, however, held at the parish, divide the parish into many small groups. Begin with groups of four or five,

where "each one brings one" so that the opportunity is given for all to speak and all to be heard. Decide, as groups, how the concerns expressed can be returned to the larger community, and worked on by that larger community.

3. In many parishes the parents of very small children are sometimes never away from the children, or in touch with other young parents in similar circumstances. With other parents of children beginning formal religious schooling, design a series of three or four meetings to bring these parents together to speak of issues that concern them in their parenting; be sure the groups include "experienced" parents who can help with these issues. No "expert" from the parish staff is needed except perhaps to convene the meeting; the opportunity to come together is the point.

6

The Role of Model

Children learn

[*A Beginning Pause: Taking a Few Moments To Become Quiet.*

By now you may be developing the habit of taking a few moments to be quiet, to be still, in order to reflect on yourself as a person of faith, in relation to your children and to the vocation of parenting. By now your children may be noticing you doing this, and going along with you. But if your quieting pauses are not becoming part of your routine, this might be a good time to decide on a particular time of day, or day of the week, as well as a place where you will do this quieting, and build it into the family schedule.

Today, after you have become still, take the next several minutes to reflect on the following questions:

Does anyone who knows you ever remark that you are just "like" someone else in your family—perhaps a generation ahead of you? Who? In what ways is the resemblance perceived?

How do you think someone becomes "like" another person?

Are there people you would wish you were like? Who are they? Why do you wish you could be like them?

When you think of the way you pray, or your attitudes toward church and God, where did you learn them? How?

When you think of the people who are your best friends, can you say what about them drew you to them in the first place? Not only *how*, but *why* did you become friends?

Is there anything in your life now that you hope your children will imitate?

Is there anything in your life you hope your children will avoid?

Is there anything you can do either to foster the imitation or to make sure it won't happen?

Do you ever think of yourself as a "role model" for your children? If so, can you put into words, "spin out" what that might mean?]

One of the best-known and most powerful, anti-smoking TV spots was made years ago. A father walks through the woods, followed by his lively—and precious—three year old son. The father picks up a stick; the little boy does the same. The father skims a rock across the surface of a lake; the little boy does the same. The father sits down on the grass, his back against a tree; so does the child. And then the father reaches out his hand, picks a cigarette out of a pack, and puts it in his mouth. The spot ends with the boy reaching out his hand too—and with a voice-over asking, "Like father, like son?"

Much is written, in the press and in research literature, about the idea of the "role model." Harvard Law School, for example, recently became involved in a crisis between administration, faculty and students, over the hiring of a black woman teacher: the argument made was that students who were black women needed a "role model" to demonstrate what it was like to be a black female involved in the practice of law; but other students needed that modeling too, to represent the fullness of the human community. Athletes, discovered to be using drugs, are regularly given heightened media coverage, their habit lamented because they are "role models" for the young people of our society. And teenagers throughout the world routinely dress in the same way as their most popular musical idols, who are presumably, in some way, also "role models."

The idea of some of us modeling ways of behaving and thinking for others is not a new one. In religious traditions, the lives of the saints, and of those ancestors we want to memorialize, are the basis of story after story, in large part so that we can learn how to imitate them. Elie Wiesel captures the power of such story-telling in telling of the Jewish search to know the Hasidic masters. He says quite simply that all of us, with one another—whether famous or unknown—are always asking, "Where does your life tell me about my life?"

Where does your life tell me about my life? Of no one is this question asked more than of parents; by no one is it asked more than by their children. The irony of this particular question between parents and children, however, is that it is rarely, if ever, asked directly. Instead, the asking and the answering are indirect. The modeling that goes on is at a deeper, more profound and more powerful level than that of simple question and answer. But there is a second irony. At the same time modeling is indirect, it is also direct. Let us look at these apparent opposites.

51

Indirect Modeling. It is fairly likely that no one *consciously* acts as a "role model" for someone else, in the sense of "I will be a role model for so-and-so, and he or she will copy or imitate what I do." In this, being a model is a great deal like dancing. The more you look at your feet, the more likely you are to stumble. The fancy footwork involved in the dance of the role model is that the more genuine it is the more *un*intended it is. A Buddhist teaching puts this well:

> How hard you search for it
> You will never be able to grasp it.
> You can only become it.

Complicating this role even further is the discovery that our children often learn what we consciously intend they *not* learn! So it is worth taking time to reflect on how modeling goes on indirectly in daily life and in the area of religious faith.

A first form of modeling is speech—not the actual words, so much as *how* they are said. A three year old, asked by her mother to put down her blanket and come to have breakfast, responds, "But Mommy, I just can't function in the morning without my blanket!" Presumably the child does not know the meaning of "function." But she *has* heard the tone her mother uses and the entire sentence enough times to substitute the word "blanket" for the word "coffee." Indeed, in the beginning of life, children learn to speak by imitating patterns of speech, and not individual words.

This imitation of patterns is particularly important when parents speak about other people. The child picks up, by a kind of human osmosis, those feelings lying behind the words that are said. (Just think for a moment about table conversations where sex is the issue, and how the entire tone often changes when children are present.) And they learn that words can be either extraordinarily damaging or extraordinarily healing. Expressions such as "She can't help it, poor soul," or "He means well," although clichés, also embody attitudes toward others. This can be of critical importance when speaking is about entire races or ethnic groups. It is where the primary command to "Love your neighbor as yourself" is modeled—or not modeled.

Similarly, parents' attitudes toward prayer, church and God are conveyed more by what the adults do than by what they say. If our children observe us regularly stopping to pray, or regularly attending church, we convey this is important to us, and important to adult life. But they also tie such practice to daily life over the long haul. I remember once meeting a woman who talked about her father with utmost reverence. She said of him, "My father was not a churchgoer. Actually, he ran a small store in the poor neighborhood where we lived. But though he didn't go to church much, what I remember is the way he treated his customers. No one ever went hungry because one couldn't pay. He was a deeply religious man."

Direct Modeling. By a strange paradox, however, modeling *can* be direct. This is especially true when the modeling is done by the community, or by parents as members of a larger group than the family alone. And this is where the power of the church as a tradition can be felt most fully, and where the power of belonging to a people enters the deepest part of the human self. For despite all its faults and flaws, the church has built into its life, over centuries, ways of acting and behaving that children see and experience as *necessary* ways of acting and behaving. The first way is in handing on a story; the second is in facing the major moments in life, especially the moment of death.

In the church's liturgy, over and over, the story is told of one who was born, lived, suffered, died and rose from the dead. It is a story that at first unconsciously, but then more consciously, becomes our personal story too, as we age. The story is told on a yearly basis, from Advent through Christmas, toward Lent and into Easter. It is followed, again yearly, by the long—and sometimes lazily boring—time after Pentecost that culminates with the assumption and the feast of Christ the King, leading us into the beginning of the story once again. But it is also told on a daily basis, in the simplicity of daily mass, daily prayer, and careful readings from scripture, designed to embody the story being told in the wider liturgical year.

Equally powerful is the church modeling the importance of the significant moments of human life, and offering rituals that convey to a child—and its parents—the need to celebrate and memorialize, the need to lift up the critical times. The funeral mass and burial, for example, can be a great resource for a child losing a grandparent, and even more so for a child who loses a parent. It is a way of saying that the person who has died has joined a company of others, is not forgotten, and will rise again, reborn, someday. The baptism of a new brother or sister is a way of saying: "Welcome to the world. You will not be alone; we are your people." Confirmation, and orders, and marriage are ways of saying: "Here is a new time in your life; grasp it fully, and live into it with our best wishes." Reconciliation is a way of saying: "You've made a mistake, yes; but now is a time to start over." And perhaps most powerfully, the sacrament of eucharist, received for the first time by six, seven and eight year olds, is a way of saying to both a child and its parents: "Here is bread for you to eat: bread for the life of the world. Through it you are nourished, renewed and reborn. For the body of the Christ, broken yet given, models a way of living. It models a way of being so that you, too, may become life for the world."

wow!

FOR FURTHER EXPLORATION

1. "One day I looked in the mirror, and saw my mother's face." "One day I put on my jacket, and saw my father's hand come through the sleeve." Take time, with a group of adults, to think together on what these sayings might mean. Then move on to explore what it might mean to discover God's face in the mirror looking back at us, God's hand grasping ours.

2. With your children, try to discover rituals you live, as a family, that you received from your parents, their grandparents—for example, birthday parties, going-to-bed stories, naming goldfish. Ask them which ones are their favorites, and why. Then decide on a new ritual you might want to create for yourselves as a family.

55

3. Go through your house and look at the pictures of people, including those of rock stars that may be in your teenagers' rooms, and those in snapshots and/or in the family album. Decide together, as a family, what all of these say about the modeling going on in your house.

7

The Roles of Women and Men

[*A Beginning Pause: Taking a Few Moments To Become Quiet.*

Go to the special place in your home that you have discovered is right for you, and again move toward stillness. This is your own special time to meditate; and even if it is as brief as ten or fifteen minutes, allow yourself to receive it as a gift. Permit yourself the luxury of doing nothing, of following your breath, of simply being *there*. Tell the children, or your spouse, you are going into your "heart room" and invite them to come with you, if they wish, and if you wish. When you experience yourself as still, take time to reflect on the following. If you are reflecting with others, let each respond to the questions and try to discover what you might learn from one another.

If you are a woman, who are the most significant women in your life? Can you pinpoint the ways in which these women contributed to your sense of yourself as a woman? If you are a man, who are the most significant men in your life? Can you pinpoint the ways in which these men contributed to your sense of yourself as a man?

How does the gender you are cause you to differ in your parenting of a daughter and your parenting of a son?

What do you believe about the roles of men and women in the family? What about girls and boys? Are they the same, different, or somewhere in between?

Do you and your spouse agree in these beliefs?

Do you believe our society treats men and women differently? If so, how? And why?

Do you believe our church treats men and women differently? If so, how? And why?

How (so far) have you explained gender differences to your children?

How do you—or do you plan to—speak with your children about their own sexuality?

What do you think you model to your children about being male? About being female?

What do you think the church models to your children about being male? About being female?]

"Dear God," writes Sylvia, "are boys better than girls? I know you are one, but try to be fair."

"Dear God, Father of Jesus," writes Bruce, "how does it feel to be the biggest, best dad in the whole United States? You must make out okay on Father's day."

"Dear Mr. and Mrs. God," writes Karen, "what's your family like? Is Jesus the oldest?"

"Dear God," writes Hank, "what is the rest of the story about when you made boys and girls? There must be a reason why you made two different brands of people."

From the beginning, whether their questions are as tiny as themselves, or as big as God, children are aware of differences in being boys and being girls, in being women and being men. No surprise, of course; a baby's gender is the first question asked when we have news of a birth. But worldwide, as the twentieth century ends, the human community is in the midst of attending to gender differences in ways that are unprecedented.

Women are not alone in this attending: men too are asking questions concerning what it is to be male in this society—personal questions, yes, but also questions related to war, and work, and ecology. In the church, questions on sexuality (abortion; contraception; celibacy; homosexuality) and on the ordination of women continue to be central topics, and often tear congregations apart. Many younger people are disaffected from the church because of what they perceive to be negative attitudes toward women and toward married men who might wish to be priests. And, as the letters from Sylvia, Bruce, Karen and Hank indicate, and as we saw in Chapter 3, even gender-related images of God are up for consideration.

Given all of this, it has become crucial for parents to reflect not only on their roles as parents, and as role models, as we did in the last two chapters, but also on the roles they find they are asked to play, in society and in the church, as women and as men. For the way we *are* as men, and as women, and even more what we convey to our children about *themselves* as male or female, are major factors influencing our children's sense of what it is to be boy or girl, woman or man.

One of the most startling discoveries about this same-sex influence comes from recent research on the development of girls, done in several cities throughout the United States. Although the number of girls studied is relatively small, the data collected thus far suggests that somewhere around age twelve girls suffer a developmental loss. The loss is particularly evident in what they say—and in what they don't say. Far too often, from being "spunky at two, and dauntless at five," as the little heroine of *Rebecca of Sunnybrook Farm* is described, and from being outspoken, fearless and feisty six, seven and eight years olds, girls around twelve *stop* saying what they know. And from assuming that anger, conflict and fights are all part of being human, they begin to hide such feelings in order to be considered "nice."

For our purpose in this chapter, the findings are important because the major hunch concerning *why* this occurs in so many girls' lives is that the age of twelve is the age when girls begin identifying with adult women! And so it becomes a central concern for mothers—and fathers—to keep their daughters' voices alive if parts of their daughters are not to go underground, if parts of their daughters are not swallowed up by images of "the perfect girl"—the girl too often presented, especially by religion, as the perfect girl: nice, never mean, and "good" to the core.

Obviously, we need to have data about what is happening to boys in this era as well. We do know that although more male babies are born each year in this society (106 to 100), fewer males survive past the first six months. In fact, during the first year of life, the male death rate is one third higher than that for girl babies. James Nelson, who has studied male sexuality and its relation to masculine spirituality, suggests that part of the reason for these statistics is that baby boys are treated differently from baby girls, too often receiving less touch, less physical nurture. We also know that boys are slower in developing positive body images than girls are, and that boys are pressured against "effeminacy" from their earliest years because of the still strong bias against homosexuality.

Such discoveries are coming to the fore as male-female roles—especially in relation to one another—continue to change: as fathers become "house-husbands," for example, or become more mutually responsible for child-care than they have been, and as images of men as tender, gentle and caring become more accepted, and "macho" no longer defines the perfect man.

Given such changes, parents are forced, inevitably, to attend to the power they have before their children in modeling manhood and in modeling womanhood. Some are looking twice at the "givens" only recently noticed: why all their daughters' things are pink, and all their sons' are blue; why girls' toys and boys' toys are separated in department stores; why the girls wash the dishes and the boys take out the garbage (or have no household chores, because those are things girls do!); why such teachings exist, for example, as the ones that girls don't get messed up and boys don't cry.

Such examination spills over into the church as well. Most adults, at least in the U.S. church, are looking at official church attitudes toward sexuality, toward the roles of women and men, and being honest in voicing what they see as sins of sexism and heterosexism. Even among the youngest children, sometimes especially among the youngest children, neither boys nor girls are likely to accept as convincing the argument, with reference to no altar girls, or not ordaining women or mar-

61

ried men, or toward not acknowledging the reality of lesbian and gay persons' lives, that "this is the way it's always been."

Further—and this is where such issues come back home—parents have begun to examine their own attitudes, prejudices and fears in the area of sexuality, an area where most adults still feel some discomfort. Women have developed a number of skills during the last two decades in facing women's issues together; men are beginning to meet—in much smaller numbers, true—to face together the meaning of masculinity in church and society, and to be honest about their fears and feelings concerning sexuality.

The importance of such work cannot be stressed too much: not only because of its impact on young children, but because of its impact on parents' developing *spiritually* as well as sexually. For the yearning that both women and men experience today for closeness, fulfillment and intimacy—for wholeness—can be understood as a yearning for God. It can be understood as a movement toward the center, toward the mystery who sustains us all. It can be understood as a journey toward a connection not only with all that is, but toward the one who created all that is, and found it good.

FOR FURTHER EXPLORATION

1. Find out if there are any men's groups, or women's groups in your church, studying the issues raised in this chapter. If there are, discuss why you might or might not join them. If there aren't, discuss why you might or might not start one.

2. Take a look around your own home, with your children, for signs of how maleness and femaleness are imaged: in toys, pictures, chores—of both adults and children—in responsibility toward grandparents, in prayers. Have a discussion together on how you feel about these signs, and on whether you feel any of them might be changed.

3. *Reading Resources:* The following are some recent books on female and male differences, sexuality, and/or spirituality that you might like to read, either alone or as part of a parents' reading group:

Bianchi, Eugene and Rosemary Ruether. *From Machismo to Mutuality.* New York: Paulist Press, 1976.

Bly, Robert. *Iron John.* Reading: Addison-Wesley, 1990.

Gerzon, Mark. *A Choice of Heroes. The Changing Faces of American Manhood.* Boston: Houghton Mifflin Co., 1982.

Gilligan, Carol. *In a Different Voice.* Cambridge: Harvard University Press, 1982.

Gilligan, Carol, Nona P. Lyons and Trudy J. Hammer (eds.). *Making Connections. The Relational Worlds of Adolescent Girls at Emma Willard School.* Cambridge: Harvard University Press, 1990.

Gilligan, Carol, Jane Victoria Ward and Jill McLean Taylor (eds.) with Betty Bardige: *Mapping the Moral Domain. A Contribution of Women's Thinking to Psychological Theory and Education.* Cambridge: Harvard University Press, 1988.

Harris, Maria. *Dance of the Spirit: The Seven Steps of Women's Spirituality.* New York: Bantam Books, 1989.

Nelson, James B. *Embodiment.* Minneapolis: Augsburg
Press, 1978.

Nelson, James B. *The Intimate Connection. Male Sexuality, Masculine Spirituality.* Philadelphia: The Westminster Press, 1988.

Ruddick, Sara. *Maternal Thinking.* Boston: Beacon Press,
1989.

8

The Role of Adult

[*A Beginning Pause: Taking a Few Moments To Become Quiet.*

Sit back in your soul. As you know by now, the way to sit back in your soul is to sit back in your spirit. Attend to your breath: let it become deeper and slower. Attend to your body, too, and allow your body to accompany your breathing, alert to feelings of calm as you begin to be centered. The quieting time for this chapter is an opportunity to reflect on what we know about adulthood, especially adult faith: what that faith is for us, and how it may have an impact on our children.

When you hear the word "adult," what are some of the *qualities* or *characteristics* that come to your mind?

In what ways do you personally express or embody these characteristics?

In what ways do you find yourself needing to develop at least one or two of them still further?

Do you remember how you felt and thought about "grown-ups" in your childhood? Did you want to grow up? Or did you wish you could stay six, or eight, or ten forever?

Who are people who model the meaning of "adulthood" to you now? Can you say why you choose them?

Who are people who modeled the meaning of

"adulthood" to you when you were a child? Again, can you say why?

Are there people you didn't much like—or perhaps did not understand—when you were a child, but who, you now realize, were full, complete and strong as adults?

Are there people you liked a great deal when you were a child, but who, you suspect, have still not grown up completely?

What's the best thing about being an adult?

What's the worst?

Would you say our church is an "adult" church? If so, why? If not, why not?]

Among the most poignant aspects of any society are children who have grown up too quickly, who have never known childhood—or, worse, will never know it. Circumstances have forced them to take over adult duties, at home, or in their societies, before their time. We might think here of children who raise siblings because a parent has died, who go off to war as boys, sometimes lying about their ages, who live close to death from hunger in the arms of their parents, in Bombay or Ethiopia or parts of our own country.

Less immediately a focus of our sympathy, but tragic in its own way, are adults who have never grown up. And even worse are systems and structures and institutions that prevent the move to adulthood—systems, structures and institutions that, by their attitudes and treatment of adults, suggest that "Big Daddy," or "Big Mama," knows best.

In this chapter, where we consider the role of adult, we will look at some meanings and examples of what genuine adulthood is. Then we will focus on adult faith, especially its implications for children. Finally we will look at how the church as a whole, and individual parishes, can be places that develop the adulthood of their people and, as parishes, mirror the meaning of an adult community.

Genuine Adulthood. It may come as a surprise to learn that until recently adulthood was not much studied by psychologists. Where *child* psychologists and *adolescent* psychologists have been with us for almost a century, attention has been directed only in the past few decades to the meaning of genuine adulthood. And, as we saw in the last chapter, changing roles of men and women have even affected the smaller number of research results we do have.

One major shift in understanding genuine adulthood stands out. This is the change from assuming "adult" means rational, logical, independent, and capable of making judgments, in contrast to being playful, non-rational—not irrational—artistic, and dependent. This playing off of one set of qualities against the other was quite popular in the recent past, and even got bestseller status in a book called *I'm O.K.; You're O.K.* that taught, implicitly, that adults and parents were not the same! (People said to each other, "That's your parent talking," when one person seemed to be ordering another around, or "That's your adult talking," when the other was being overly logical, or not showing emotion.)

The change is not a move in favor of the second set of qualities over the first—for example, being playful as better and more adult than being rational, or being spontaneous better than being serious and planning ahead. Rather, it is the realization that adulthood is a *combination* of characteristics; adults are people who are able to be both serious *and* playful, artistic *and* logical. Genuine adults combine dependence and independence in order to be *interdependent:* with other human beings and with the air and the water and the earth. Genuine adults are those who know that although we must make judgments, we also need each other's help and counsel in making them. Genuine adults are able to be dependently independent and independently dependent.

Adult Faith and Religious Tradition. Although this meaning of adulthood is only now being discovered by our modern world, it is a meaning found at the heart of the gospels and in Jewish and Christian tradition. Our Catholicism is characterized by being a faith that not only teaches but actually *celebrates* the combining of opposites! In light there is darkness, we say, and in darkness there is light; in death there is life, and in life, death; in mourning there is rejoicing, and in joy there is always sorrow. Even more astonishing, we teach that in Jesus, and in ourselves, God is human; and in humanity we find God. Divinity is part of humanity; humanity is part of divinity.

To talk about opposites is easy; to live in the midst of them is difficult. But it is this living in the midst of contradiction, this living both in death and the hope of resurrection, that equals the gift of adult faith parents can give children. For this is precisely where adults *differ* from children. The child sees in black and white; the adult sees the reality of gray. The child believes questions *have* answers; the adult knows life is a journey that generally poses questions to answers. Most of the time these ways of faith and believing go unspoken. But in the painful times: of suffering, illness, death and loss, adult faith is sustaining faith. In the joyful times, adult faith stops to celebrate. When happiness rains down as a free gift, adults do not think it evil to sing and rejoice. And when no answers are forthcoming, adults know how to live in the midst of questions, even learning, as the poet Rilke said, to "love the questions themselves like locked rooms" and eventually to live into whatever answers are possible.

Toward an Adult Church. From what is said above, it could seem that what I have called the "genuine" adult is someone who has achieved the perfect balance in the integration of opposite qualities. It could seem that a time comes when one "reaches" adulthood. But that is not the case. The journey toward adulthood is lifelong, and rare is the person who embodies the ideal in actual practice. Not even the greatest saints have achieved perfect adulthood. But that is precisely where the church comes in, and why a community like the church is necessary.

For what the church—as a people—*does* do is take up the slack. In the hard times when my faith is low, or nil, or apparently non-existent, I need not fear. Instead, I can call on the faith of the community to bear me up, to hold my hands, to make sure I do not sink when despair threatens. The community has the living hope that may be in short supply for me at the moment. Later on, when my faith becomes stronger, I can place it at the disposal of those sisters and brothers who are going through their own bad times.

Or when I am undergoing the mourning and the

grieving that accompany the death of a spouse, or a child, or a parent, I do not need to "keep a stiff upper lip." The community can do that for me, and allow me to take the necessary human time I need not only to grieve my loss, but to "rage against the dying of the light."

At a more practical, or programmatic level, the local church might enrich adult faith in ways that benefit the next generation by giving more attention to intergenerational experiences, so that across age lines people learn from one another. Often the first thing we think of here are formal programs in schooling. But it might be wise to begin, instead, by looking around to see where intergenerational experiences are already going on, or where they might occur with little shift in either resources or personnel. A men's choir, for example, in adding boys or a women's choir adding girls is one such avenue. People in groups of three families at a time planning Sunday liturgies each week is another. Hospitality committees that bring food to the sick or elderly, or care for the children of parents who may be away, is another. And freeing young parents to come together—as suggested at the end of Chapter 5—may be accomplished easily in the parish that brings its oldest members together with the small children, as the young parents are meeting. Such works, while assisting adults in companioning one another, are also opportunities for children to see the many varieties of adult faith.

But most of all, at an official level, the church can be a place of listening. Although any organization wants to pass on its ways of doctrine and ways of behaving—received from the past—this is only one of its many reasons for being. If it wants to foster the adulthood of its present membership, it must begin by taking them seriously as grown-ups, and trusting their own treasury of wisdom, built up throughout life. In doing such listening, and refusing to always be the one who speaks—or speaks first—the church's own adulthood will itself be revitalized into the next century.

FOR FURTHER EXPLORATION

1. With your children, check out the "adult" quotient of characters in your favorite TV programs. Try to decide together who seem to have the most "adult" qualities, even if they are children. Get in the habit of evaluating who is acting like a "real" grown-up.

2. Sketch a time line of your own adulthood, at five year periods, starting with your birth. At each five year marker, draw a symbol that represents at least the beginning of an "adult" quality in your life (even if you were chronologically a child). Finally, "draw" a conclusion describing you—and your spouse, if possible—in adulthood at present.

5	10	15	20	25

30	35	40	45 etc.

A symbol expressing the adult you: _____

3. Read either the novel *Ordinary People* (Guest), the novel *The Plague* (Camus), the novel *The Color Purple* (Walker), or the novel *Cat's Eye* (Atwood). In your journal, if you keep one, talk about what the novel teaches children about adulthood or about adult faith.

Part Three: Resources

One of the great secrets of adult life is the revelation that we do not have to do it alone. No matter what the "it" is: cooking, swimming, loving—or, as in this book, parenting—resources exist all around us: to awaken us, to comfort us when we are discouraged, to keep us from making dumb mistakes. Some of these resources are small ones: a book, a recipe, an electric can opener, a phone call. But some of them are mighty and ancient.

The mighty, ancient resources are the subjects of the four chapters in this section. They are *mighty* because they are sources of power, and because if we incorporate them into our personal and familial lives, they will disclose an energy for us we did not know was there. They are *ancient* because they have been part of the treasury of the human community for millennia, tried, true, always capable of being renewed. The resources are art and sport, story and storytelling, spirituality, and community.

As we turn our attention to them, we begin, as we have previously, with a brief opportunity to be still and to ponder some questions about our relation with each of the resources. A brief commentary follows. Finally, each chapter concludes with suggestions for ways we might explore the particular resource in order to make it part of our lives.

9

Art and Sport as Resources

[*A Beginning Pause: Taking a Few Moments To Become Quiet.*

As you begin this last section of *The Faith of Parents* and consider resources that might deepen your own and your children's religious lives, take a few moments to become still. Attend to your breath: inhale, exhale . . . inhale, exhale . . . inhale, exhale at least seven times, counting on the exhaled breath from one to seven. "Inhale . . . exhale one . . .; inhale . . . exhale two . . .; inhale . . . exhale three," etc. As you feel yourself becoming calmer and more still, reflect quietly on the following questions, either alone, with your spouse, or with a group of other parents like yourself.

Does music have a place in your life and that of your family? If it does, can you say how that began? If it doesn't, do you have any understanding why it doesn't?

Do you, or does anyone in your family, paint or draw? Are any of you particularly good at creating symbols or images? Again, if there are, can you say more about that? And if there aren't, do you have any sense of why not?

What about dance, or drama, or photography, or film, or sculpting of some sort?

As you look around your home, what if any signs of

art do you notice? What does the design of your home say about your relation to art and the arts?

Do you play a particular sport: basketball, baseball, tennis? Does anyone in your family engage in a sport, either alone (swimming or running, for example), or on a team?

Do you enjoy watching sports?

Do you play any sport together with your children?

If you don't have contact with art or sport in some form, do you feel something is missing?]

The story is told of a wise rabbi who was invited to travel to a far-off place to bring peace to its feuding townspeople. When he arrived it was market day, and the marketplace was crowded. The rabbi walked straight toward the center of things and began to sing a bright, happy tune. So happy was his song that many joined the singing, first one by one, but then in small choruses, until all were singing and the market was filled with music. Then the rabbi began dancing, first slowly, and then more quickly, clapping his hands as he did so and with such joy in his expression that people began tapping their feet. As the rabbi danced, he took the hands of one villager after another, who in turn grasped someone else, until all were dancing and singing together, and the reasons for their quarreling were forgotten.

The Arts

Music and dancing have always been part of religious life. They figure importantly in rituals, liturgies, sacraments and celebrations, performing a role that is usually not possible for language alone. Their work is, essentially, to give *form* to the human feeling, insight and experience not completely expressible through words. The arts also have the power to heal wounds, to end conflict, and to bring together that which has been broken, including people who have been separated or alienated from each other. God, the wise rabbi, gives us the arts to make us whole.

Music and dance are not the only arts, however, nor are healing and wholeness the only accomplishments of art. The arts also exist as reminders of our call to be like God in another area: creation. Throughout the Hebrew Bible, as well as the New Testament, we have many images of the creator God: separating light from darkness, and day from night, and sea from sky in the beginning in order to give us a world; giving men and women one another that we might know community and family. We also have the image of God acting as a potter, forming us from clay, fashioning us as a people. And we know something of the power this artistic work involves, when we reflect on the creator Spirit arriving on Pentecost in the form of tongues of *fire*.

As parents we are called to join God in this creative, artistic activity. Our co-creating with God is first evident in our giving life to our children. But the birth moments are actually only the beginning of our artistry: once the unlimited actions of parenting become ours, we learn we must be continually creative as each day unfolds, calling us to come up with new solutions to problems, to new ways of being together. And at some point we realize we are *shapers* and *designers* and *form-givers,* as all artists are.

The innumerable human arts can be a great resource to us in this wider, more generalized creative activity. For some of us, our great "artistic" work may be bread-baking, homemaking, gardening or carpentry; for others it may be the way we "parent." But if we want to deepen and enhance these daily, more simple artistic works, we ourselves would be wise to practice some art form and introduce our children to the arts as well: to painting, sculpture, music, photography, dance or drama, so that a realm of human life with great power for holiness and wholeness will not be lost to them. We would be wise to make some "work" of art part of our family's identity. And we would be wise to offer our children the richness of an aesthetically pleasing environment. Doing that, we would equip ourselves and our children with ways of being in the world creatively, ways available in no other form.

Sport and Play

No other form except, perhaps, for a second great resource: sport. At its best, sport is an extension of something all children know how to do—play. Actually children do not need to be taught how to play, although they can learn to play better: with discipline, so they do not give up too easily; with compassion, so that competition does not create enemies; with a "light touch," so that the game itself, rather than its outcome, is the focus of their attention. Girls need the same opportunity for play and organized sport as boys do, and through play they can come to know their own bodiliness, in its power and its limitations. Not incidentally, girls can also be given the resource of play/sport as an antidote to the eating abuses so prevalent among girls even during their childhood years.

Children will not receive the fullness of play's

graces, however, unless parents take play seriously too. This may not be through a particular sport (although it may be). But it will be demonstrated to children if their parents "play" at their work, with as much ease as possible, and with an absence of solemnity. Actually, the church has been an advocate of such approaches throughout Christian history, through the practice of designating particular days as "holy days"—where freedom from labor is seen not only as a delight, but as a commandment.

Sabbath

The religious grounding of art and sport are not always taught. But the reason they are central, holy resources is their connection with sabbath. In both Jewish and Christian history, sabbath has always been made up of three components, and in understanding them, we may see the connections with art and sport more easily.

1. *The Component of Law.* From the beginning of God's covenant with the Hebrew people, sabbath has been a primary law. Law here is not to be understood as a command or a rule: a "making do." Instead, the sabbath law is akin to such laws as gravity, or relativity: a "telling what." Sabbath, as one of the divine laws, is meant to tell us humans what we are. And in this case, sabbath is a law telling us that as humans, we are the created beings who honor the creator God by the cessation of work.

The Babylonian translation of Sabbath is *sappatu*—the time for quieting the heart. In Hebrew, the word used is *shavat*—and that means to "stop, cease, and desist" from work. In other words, sabbath teaches there are many ways to be in time and to "spend" time, and only one of these ways is through working and earning a living. We also need time for stopping, being still, and dwelling, as we can do in the works of art, as we can do through sport and play. It is a law of our being.

2. *The Component of Rest.* The book of Exodus records the sabbath command:

> Remember the sabbath day, to keep it holy. Six days you shall labor, and do all your work; but the seventh day is a sabbath to the Lord your God; in it you shall not do any work, you, or your son, or your daughter, your manservant or your maidservant, or your cattle, or the sojourner who is within your gate; for in six days the Lord made heaven and earth, the sea and all that is in them, and rested the seventh day; therefore the Lord blessed the sabbath day and hallowed it (Ex 20:8–11).

Sometimes religions have misunderstood this command as one enjoining fear and deprivation. But the rest and "not-doing" of sabbath is directed to joy, not suffering; we are given the sabbath command by our creator so that we might enjoy the delights of the universe.

A further meaning of the command to rest, however, is one that is related to action for justice in the world: not only are human beings to rest—the animals and the land are also to be given the chance to be still. What begins as a ceremonial, ritual command—to honor the rest of the creator God—is very early taken up as an ethical and moral obligation as well. *You* are to rest—and you are to be sure the rest of creation rests too—because you are its steward. Again, we should be able to see how perfectly and powerfully art and sport can be resources here. They are ways to rest our spirits as well as our bodies.

3. *The Component of Recreation in Community.* But ceasing to work and engaging in rest are not all. When we stop work, and take the time for dwelling with the creator, we are also told by sabbath to do that with one another: to come together as a people, in community (which probably led eventually to a "Sunday obligation" in Christianity). The point was, however, that if we came together as communities, we would be able to play, as our artistic creator wished, in two ways: first, through recreation—the works of festivity and parades and celebrations, and secondly through *re*-creation—the works of reforming and reshaping and redesigning the world. To use the resources of art and sport as sabbath suggests is to take them seriously as resources. It is also to fulfill the commandment of a creator God who is a wise rabbi, singing and dancing us into wholeness and happiness.

FOR FURTHER EXPLORATION

1. The next time you have a family outing, suggest that some members of the family take a sketchbook and draw/sketch the persons, places and things they want to remember rather than photographing them. If one of your children is going to be away for a while (at camp, with cousins, at school), send him or her a sketchbook and some pencils in order to do the same. Try some sketching yourself and, after doing this several times, come together to share what you may have discovered.

2. Decide that on the next six Sundays you will do no housework, no shopping, no cooking. Explain why you are doing this by discussing the three components of sabbath named in this chapter. Help each person to have enough time to prepare ahead so that the sabbath can be a genuine day of rest. Enlist everyone in the family to take part in the necessary preparations beforehand, and then have a family conference on what you have learned.

3. Play "My favorite game is . . ." with everyone in your family. Each person gets to name three or four of her or his favorite games and to tell why. When you have had conversations about this, try to design the family environment so that everyone has time for his or her favorite game at least once a week.

10

Story and Storytelling as Resources

[*A Beginning Pause: Taking a Few Moments To Become Quiet.*

As you look forward to the following ten or fifteen minutes, situate yourself in a relaxed, comfortable place. You may want to begin by lighting a candle to help you become centered. Put the candle in the center of the floor, or on a table in front of you, and give your attention to its quiet flickering. Let the candle symbolize the growing feeling of peace inside yourself. As you contemplate it, breathe deeply, from one to ten long breaths, until you feel at rest and ready to reflect on the following questions about the place of story and storytelling in your life.

When you think of your life as a story, what are the two or three central stories in your life thus far?

Are there any similarities in these stories, any common themes? Are there differences?

Are there stories in your life—stories you have lived—that you would call stories of "birth"? Are there stories of "death"? Are there stories of "resurrection"?

Think back now to your childhood. What were

some of your favorite stories when you were a child? Can you say why you chose the ones you did?

Who were some of your favorite storytellers when you were a child? Again, can you say why?

If you had to pick a favorite Bible story, what story would you choose? Can you say why, and especially whether it has some connection with your own life now or in the past?

Do you tell stories to your own children? Do you regularly read stories to them?

Have you ever known the sudden experience of realizing that not only were you involved in a story—your life—but that you yourself *were* a story? If that has happened, what was it like? If it should happen in the future, what do you expect it might be like?]

Virginia Stem Owens, the writer, says that the only time she seriously considered suicide was when she was five years old. "Every night I lay in bed," she writes, "and imagined going silently into the kitchen after everyone else was asleep, sliding the long butcher knife softly from the drawer beside the sink, and pulling it slowly and steadily across my throat."

But then she adds that she never did, and asks why, answering her own question first by saying "Fear, I suppose."

Fear, and a second, more important reason—story. Story, the other great, strong memory of that time. For even as she was having those thoughts of suicide in her small bed, her mother was reading to her, again every night, as she lay in that bed, and introducing her to the great stories in our human treasury: stories like *Black Beauty,* and *Peter Pan* and *Little Women.* And what she learned from those stories then helped her to set life and death in perspective. For the stories taught her life has a *shape;* life has beginnings, endings, turns, returns. Life has ups and downs, losses and triumphs. And learning of that shape to life, she realized it was true for her life too. The stories gave her to herself.

Such is something of the power of story: story is one of what Joseph Campbell calls the "masks of God." Stories are ways of understanding the mystery and the divinity in the midst of everything, suggests Campbell, because when they are strong enough they do four things for us: 1. they leave us with the experience of *awe;* 2. they give us our place in the *cosmos,* helping us to situate ourselves in relation to the universe; 3. they name our place in the midst of *human society;* 4. they are entry points for understanding our own inner lives, *our own psychology.* Actually, when we encounter a great story, we find that it encounters us too. We find we do not stand at a distance from it; instead, we discover that it is part of the human vocation to live inside story, just as it is story's vocation to live inside us!

Our own religious heritage is founded on the power of story, the Jewish story that begins with the creation, and the Christian story that met that older story two thousand years ago. Both of those stories continue into our own day, generally under the heading "tradition"— Jewish tradition and Christian tradition. If we want our children to receive their complete inheritance, we must work to make these stories part of their lives.

First are the stories of the Hebrew Bible, what many Christians refer to as the "Old Testament." These include the "In the beginning" stories, like those found in the book of Genesis (which of course means "beginning"). They give us tales of the beginning of the world, the beginning of the human race, the beginning-again of Noah and the flood, and the beginning journey of Abraham and Sarah that led eventually to the beginnings of the Jews as a people, more especially the chosen people. These also include the stories of liberation and freedom, like those found in the book of Exodus, that give us the story of the release from slavery in Egypt, and the power of Passover, and the move through the wilderness in search of the promised land. The Hebrew Bible also includes the stories of great heroes and heroines who continue to influence us today, and who, in both the greatness and the limitations of their lives, remind us of their similarity with us. These are the people with names like David, Moses, Rachel, Rebecca, Judith, Esther, Daniel and Ruth.

One great characteristic of Jewish storytelling concerns people who tell stories about stories in the Bible, people called *darshanim,* as well as the stories they write about the stories in the Bible called *midrashim.* A *midrash* is the Jewish name for a story about a story in the Bible, and there are both centuries-old midrashim, and new stories told by modern rabbis. One of the finest of the new *darshanim* is Rabbi Marc Geller. Telling about Adam naming the animals, for example, he describes Adam naming them first by numbers: "1, 2, 3, 4, etc." are their names. Then Adam runs out of numbers and decides to call all the animals by the same name, "Hey you!" That doesn't work either, and eventually Adam gets smart and asks the animals themselves what their names are. They answer immediately, just as we might, because we know who we are, in all our personal, unique selfhood.

Rabbi Geller also tells of the angels asking if the

creation were finished yet, and being referred to human beings by God with the cryptic answer, "Ask my partners." He tells of Noah's sadness in having to leave so many of his friends behind. He tells of how Adam and Eve eventually left the garden, because they were lured by the need of a dying tomato plant. And in offering these stories, these *midrashim,* he sends us back to the original stories, ever ancient and ever new, found in the Bible.

The Christian New Testament is the other great treasury of our religious stories. Here the stories center around the person of Jesus and his apostles and disciples, as well as around the people he met or influenced during his life: Martha, Mary, the rich young man, Zacchaeus. The stories also center around the story-form Jesus loved so much, the parable, a form that has given us characters like the prodigal son, the woman searching for the lost coin, and the good shepherd, and images like the mustard seed and the vine and the branches. In addition, the New Testament is filled with miracle stories too, addressing the wondrous, amazing, marvelous aspects of Emmanuel—God with us.

The primary story of the New Testament, however, is the one sacramentalized and memorialized and told and retold liturgically every year: the story of the birth, childhood, growing-up, public life, suffering, death and rising of Jesus. This great story is told and retold at Christmas and Easter, and without our realizing it becomes part of our own lives too. It emerges as our central *myth* (a story that is not only true, but more-than-true, greater-than-true), giving us the *shape* of our lives. For we too are, and live, and embody stories of birth, growing-up, public life, suffering, death and rising. In

87

knowing this story, like the child who considered suicide, we can be saved from despair and claim the religious form of our own lives.

Given such resources, what guidelines might assist parents who seek to tell the biblical stories (and other stories too) to their children? Allow me to suggest five.

1. With J.R.R. Tolkien, the author of *The Hobbit* series, adults must learn to restory themselves.

> I think children need less convincing of the importance of story than do adults. To be adult has come to mean to be adulterated . . . and to shun such childishness as we find in fairy stories. . . . So the first task, as I see it, is restorying the adult—the teacher, and the parent, and the grandparent—in order to restore the imagination, the primary place of consciousness in each of us, regardless of age.

2. Set aside time in the family schedule to tell stories: either at bedtime, or when on a journey (this can be planned for beforehand) or on one particular evening of the week.

3. After Sunday liturgy—or perhaps before—search out the fuller meaning of the stories read from and as holy scripture during worship time together. Often these passages are very brief, too brief, and we lose their full impact.

4. Get some good books of Bible stories (some are listed below), read them, and share them with your children.

5. Don't be afraid to engage in midrash, or to retell a story, or even to reject one. Some Bible stories, especially those that appear to support slavery, or the viola-

tion of women, or the killing of the innocent, must be retold, even rejected.

Doing these things should get us started on the great work of storytelling, if we have not yet begun, and encourage us to continue if we have. For these are resources too precious to be lost, too powerful to be forgotten. They are clues to who we are, who we have been, and who we might yet become.

FOR FURTHER EXPLORATION

1. As a personal exercise, for fifteen minutes at least three times a week, dwell with, stay with, and pray over one of the central life stories you named in the beginning meditation. What might this story reveal to you of who you were, who you are now, and who you hope to be, especially in relation to your children?

2. Talk with your family about the stories in their lives that
   (a) fill them with awe;
   (b) help them see their relation to the cosmos;
   (c) give them their place in society;
   (d) give them a sense of their own, unique selves.
   Try in some way to make these stories part of family celebrations, such as births, sacraments, weddings, holidays.

3. As a follow-up to some of the resources named in this chapter look for the following:

Bausch, William J. *Storytelling, Imagination and Faith.* Mystic: Twenty-Third Publications, 1984.

Geller, Marc. *Does God Have a Big Toe?* New York: Harper and Row Junior Books, 1989.

Graham, Lorenz. *How God Fix Jonah.* New York: Reynal and Hitchcock, 1948.

Ramshaw, Elaine. "The Best of the Bible Story Books for Children," in PACE 19, pp. 153–156 (February 1990), and pp. 235–239 (May 1990).

Look for Arch books, on Bible themes, produced by Concordia Publishing House (Lutheran Church Missouri Synod) usually available at Christian bookstores at $2 apiece!

11

Spirituality as Resource

[*A Beginning Pause: Taking a Few Moments To Become Quiet.*

The time is now, the place is here—to draw back from hurry and involvement and busyness as much as you can, at least for the next several minutes. Take the phone off the hook; ask the rest of the family to help you be quiet, letting them know they may join you if that's what you'd like. Ask for God's help, too, with a silent repeating of a centering word or phrase, such as "Now . . . now . . . now," or "Listen . . . listen . . . listen," or "Come, Holy Spirit . . ." Allow the word to ride on your breath, and your breath to ride on it, and feel the slowing down of your mind and your pulse as you pay attention to the resource of spirituality.

If someone asked you whether you had a spirituality, what would you be inclined to answer?

What meanings or understandings of spirituality would underlie your response?

If you said yes, has your spirituality changed over the years, and if so, why do you think that is so? If it seems not to have changed, why not?

If you say you do *not* have a spirituality, what do you believe are the reasons?

Has your parish offered help in deepening your spirituality, in developing it?

What about our culture, and our society, as helps or barriers to spirituality?

Do you want your children to have a deepened understanding and practice of spirituality? If so, what might you do as a parent to foster that?]

For anyone brought up as a Catholic Christian, spirituality is probably a familiar word. Most Catholics, even if they did not go to parochial schools, learned the word as part of their religious vocabulary, along with "grace" and "sacrament" and "priest" and "Mass." In our time, however, the word is on everyone's lips. It is spoken not only by religious people, but by people who would not identify with any religion, or even think of themselves as *against* religion. Today, spirituality is big business.

Meanings of Spirituality

Gabriel Moran points out that when spirituality began to reemerge as central to the wider society back in the late 1960s, it actually described two almost opposite movements. One was based on looking at spirituality as withdrawal, as leaving the world, as dropping out, perhaps to find a commune in the hills or a little farm where people could grow their own vegetables. In this first view, the world was too much with us, and one had to leave it in order to remain sane.

The second view of spirituality, however, came from people working in pursuit of justice: to end the war, to save the earth, to overthrow oppressive systems, to care for the world's children, especially the poorest ones. This second view was a movement not to the edge, or the periphery, as the first was, but toward the center. This second view was—and is—based on the conviction that one finds God, and human community, not by going "higher" or "farther" away. One finds God, and human community, by a movement toward the center: by going deeper into the midst of everything that exists, believing that the sacred abides at the heart of the universe; and that God is "the beyond in our midst."

This second view of spirituality is the one proposed as a resource in this chapter. Put most simply, spirituality is nothing more—and nothing less—than *our way of being in the world in the light of the mystery of God.* We need not leave the world to engage in spirituality; we need not stop doing whatever we are doing. The fidelity, hope and love that center us in this time and this place, and among these people, can fuel whatever we are doing and act as support for our own personal holiness.

The Practice of Spirituality

Many ancient practices are associated with spirituality and can serve to enhance our way of being in the world. These are practices that human beings of every religion have evolved over the centuries, practices found throughout the world. These practices are not *equal* to spirituality; nevertheless, they are the ways the human community has nourished spirituality (however it has been named) through the centuries. Often these practices are called *disciplines.* Some are personal; some are communal; some are integrating.

1. Among the *personal* disciplines, the primary one is

93

prayer—so fundamental that it is often assumed to be synonymous with spirituality. We probably pray more than we think we do: an informal "God help us" is, for all its informality, still a prayer. But prayer is generally understood as enriching our lives when we pause (1) to adore God, acknowledging we did not create the world, (2) to thank God, acknowledging that all is gift, all that is ours has come from elsewhere, including our own lives, (3) to ask divine help, acknowledging we are needy creatures, and (4) to ask forgiveness of God: for our lack of love, our lack of freedom, our refusal to be whole.

Prayer is not the only personal discipline, however; others we are probably familiar with are contemplation, meditation, centering, journaling, fasting. Many of the opening quiet times, beginning each chapter of this book, are opportunities to practice personal spiritual discipline, in order to redirect our attention to the fuller, deeper aspects of our ways of being in the world: as parents, as adults, as men and women, in the light of the mystery of God.

2. Disciplines are *communal* when we engage in them with others. Our prayer, for example, is not only personal, it is communal too, and when we participate in community prayer, we often refer to it as liturgy, or liturgical prayer. Liturgy is a fulfillment of sabbath. Liturgy is, as we have already seen, the way we gather as a people and break the bread, share the cup, tell the story, and then go forth in spirit and in truth.

Going forth, especially to do the works of feeding the hungry, sheltering the homeless, and visiting the sick and imprisoned, is another form of communal discipline—often called by the collective name "the works of mercy." Indeed, our own time has seen a reclaiming of

94

the works of mercy as central to spirituality and part of its core. What parents may need to remember here is that much of their lives are devoted to doing exactly these works: feeding, clothing, visiting and caring for the next generation. These works are not *apart* from their spirituality; these are *a part of* their spirituality. Similarly, the going forth to a job, away from their home, either because that job helps to feed and clothe others, or because the work itself contributes to the world in some way, *is* part of the practice of spirituality. So is the going forth of a child to school in order to learn and to study, for schooling and studying are that child's *way of being in the world in the light of the mystery of God.*

3. *Integrating* disciplines are the third set of practices that can foster spirituality. Some are integrating because they bring together body and spirit—such as the practice of art, and the practice of sport, especially through play. The loving and mutual practice of sex is an integrating discipline too, serving both as a great art and as a great form of play.

Other disciplines are integrating because they bring together past and present, often healing the past by reflecting on it in the present—through healing memories, through the sacrament of reconciliation, through a simple request for and receiving of forgiveness from another person. But the present can be healed by the past as well. This happens when understanding emerges from the discipline of storytelling, especially the stories telling the lives of our mothers and fathers, our foremothers and forefathers. When we know their stories, we often discover why the present is as it is, and why we are as we are. Past and present become one.

A third integrating discipline, justice, brings together what is good with what is not yet good. Here justice means—the phrase is Matthew Fox's—"the structured struggle to share the gifts of God's good earth." This can involve everything from acting as *pro bono* lawyers, to setting up soup kitchens, to lobbying for fair labor practices. For, on the one hand, we rejoice in the goodness and gifts of the earth, but, on the other, we are aware their lack is an absence of goodness for some, especially the poor. We also realize that total goodness can't be ours personally if others of us are without the gifts that rightfully belong to them too. As parents concerned with children, this has particular meaning, because most often, in most parts of the world, children are the ones who are the victims of injustice. Without justice, the integrating discipline that seeks to remedy that by bringing together the good and the not-yet-good, our spiritualities are incomplete.

The Repair of the World

The spirituality described in this chapter can be summarized in a doctrine from Jewish tradition called *tikkun olam*—the repair of the world. According to this doctrine, when God created the world, God contracted—made the divine self smaller—in order to make room for the world, and in the void that resulted, God set vessels to be filled with creative light. The power of the divine rays was so intense that the vessels shattered. This resulted in a cosmic catastrophe which left much of the light trapped in shards, in fragments, throughout our material world. *Tikkum olam* is the process of gathering the shards and restoring them to their proper order; it is an ideal of human spirituality.

Perhaps it might serve as a model for our spirituality too, and that of our children. For we are not only God's daughters and sons; we are God's partners in repairing the world.

FOR FURTHER EXPLORATION

1. Practice the prayer of ACTS—the four elements of prayer named in this chapter: Adoration, Contrition, Thanksgiving, Supplication. Hold your life as if it were a bouquet of flowers or a bundle of pick-up-sticks. Let your life fall gently and naturally from your hands, into four parts. These four will not necessarily be the same number of years—for example, if you are twenty-eight, they will probably not be seven years each in length.

   For the first part of your life, adore the God who was God for you at that time in your life. Take your time, do not hurry, and let your adoration be full and complete. Do the same with contrition, thanksgiving and supplication. Then repeat the exercise for each section of your life.

2. Engage in the practice of justice. With your children go through the newspapers for the last week carefully. Cut out pictures of children, or grownups, needing the discipline of justice to be exercised for them. Put the pictures on the refrigerator door and try to decide as a family how you might respond.

3. In the ordinary ritual of night prayers in your home, try to remember some relative or friend from the past

whose memory might enrich your understanding of the present. Tell your children a story about the person to help them understand how he or she is part of your life or how he or she has influenced your life and your children's lives too.

12

Community as Resource

[*A Beginning Pause: Taking a Few Moments To Become Quiet.*

"I am with you always." If there is any saying of Jesus that comforted his first disciples, and continues to comfort us now, it is that promise, spoken after his resurrection. God, in Jesus, is with us always, holding us in the hollow of the divine hands.

As you begin this last meditating time, allow yourself the luxury of letting go, and letting God enfold you, circle you, hold you. Be present to the sacred presence, and let it be present to you. Let go of your cares, your worries, your anxieties. Take the next few minutes simply to *be.* Then, when you are ready, spend a few moments with the following questions.

Have you ever experienced loneliness?

Can you remember the feelings that accompanied it?

Do you remember how it ended, or how you broke through it?

How would you contrast loneliness with *community*?

Do you know the experience of community with— and within—yourself?

Are there certain persons you feel yourself connected to? Those about whom you say, "These are my people"?

Can you explore what that connection feels like, what makes it up?

Can you tell when connection with others is missing?

When you reflect on your children, do you have the sense they know themselves as in a community, or part of a community?

Are there any things you and your family regularly do that you would name as examples of being in community?

Do you feel you are a part of your local parish community?

Do you feel you are in communion with God?]

Recently I was a guest at a shower for a lovely and beloved young woman. All us guests were women, and we made up four generations: the grandmother of the groom-to-be was there, as were the mothers of the bride and groom, and the older women who had watched Maura grow up. Present too were many young women in their twenties and thirties—friends, sisters, sisters-in-law. The youngest—occasional scene-stealers—were the bride-to-be's seven and eight year old nieces: enjoying the shower like the rest of us, and looking forward to their big day as flower girls.

But the most powerful part of the shower was not really in the gifts, or the splendid food, or the beautiful and loving preparation, although those symbolized the power. The power was in the ritual, in what was *not* said. It was in the coming together *of* the generations to embody the promise: you are not entering a new life alone; you have our love and support; we are with you now and in the future; we are your people. The power was in *community*.

Community figures prominently in stories of God. James Weldon Johnson's great poem *The Creation* begins with God looking around empty space and saying, "I'm lonely; I'll make me a world," reminding us even God wants to share, to be connected. That desire gets embodied both in God's search to find a people to whom God can say, "I will be your God, and you will be my people," and in the stark and simple commentary of St. John: "The Word was made flesh and dwelt among us."

But the doctrine of the church goes even further than the stories. For the doctrine teaches not only that God *wants* community; it teaches that God *is* community. That, essentially, is the meaning of the Trinity: three in one. No less a theologian than St. Thomas Aquinas points this out: "Only those things can be said to be of one essence which have one being. So the divine unity is better described by saying that the three persons are of one essence." That trinitarian formulation is open to new expression in every age, for example, "Creator, Sustainer, Spirit," in contrast to "Father, Son, Holy Ghost." But the one expression that seems to transcend the centuries is that God is not just one sacred mystery: God is one-sacred-mystery-who-is-three: God *is* community.

If it is true that we human beings are in the image of God, then that symbol of community is also ours. We too are called to be in community; we too *are* community. So back at that shower, we were not only being ourselves; we were being our godselves; we were being like God. Because we were acting as a community, we were making God present.

The Family As Community

The word "connection" has a pristine relation to community. That is because the family's first way of being community is in offering connection to its members: the connection with past generations, with a particular ethnic group, racial heritage, national identity; the connection with the rest of the family: brothers and sisters who are mother's original family, or "family of origin," brothers and sisters who are dad's. The family is the place where we receive our name and begin the lifelong journey toward discovering who we are, even if we are adopted, and not biological children. The family anchors us in the midst of a people. For parents raising children alone, this connectedness needs particular attention, and aunts and uncles and cousins assume even more prominence, as does the need for other "aunts" and "uncles" than those related solely by blood.

The connection offered by the family is particularly important in the face of sorrow. I can remember my own eight year old self, devastated by the sudden death of my too young father, asking my mother over and over, "But what will we do?" And over the years I have realized—as others like me have realized—that what we had to do was depend on—and, even more, call on—the promises implicitly made by the family community in rituals years before—rituals of shower and wedding and christening and birthday celebrations: "You have our love and support; we are with you now and in the future; we are your people."

Most of the time, however, in the daily give and take of family life, the community dimension is unspoken. But it is implicit, primarily in the family providing—and being—"home." Poet Robert Frost put it memorably: "Home is the place where, when you have to go there, they have to take you in." Home is the place you go first, with both your successes and your failures. The "A" on the exam; making the team; getting promoted—we can't wait to get home to share the news, because that's where they care most. But home is also the place that can heal through offering solitude in a room of one's own, can heal by offering the silence that knows not to probe too deeply. It is the place where the people can wait, without hurry or interruption if they are wise, until the pain can be spoken.

The Family in Community

The kind of support and connectedness a family provides is generally hard to realize if the family itself is not in community with other communities—particularly true, the smaller the unit is, for example, a one-parent, one-child unit. And so "community as resource," the focus of this last chapter, refers also to those communities outside the family that act in Godlike ways to provide connection, support and the experience of hospitality. We not only need the family *as* community; we need the family *in* community—with other communities who may be both like and unlike itself.

Parents of children with mental retardation or other

disabilities provide a remarkable illustration of this need for outside community. Because a child with disabling conditions is frequently met with silence at birth, and because our society holds up an ideal of mental and physical perfection, such parents need connection with others like themselves, others who realize that although a child may have a more obvious disability than the rest of society—where all of us have our own, more private ones—the meeting point with the child is not the child's disability, but the child's own unique self. Less obvious, but equally important, however, is what such a child and such a family contribute to other communities—what such children and such families can teach others about fidelity, hope and love.

With such families, and with those who have other needs, the parish can act as an intermediary community, a kind of broker, bringing people together. Young, unmarried adults, for example, are often delighted to be brought together with young families, and with young children, with whom they may be in contact only rarely. Newly arrived immigrants, or people having difficulty with the English language, can be introduced, in a parish, to those who might help. Those who have job or employment needs—both as employers and as employees—may use the parish as a bridge between the world of work and the world of religion.

As we have seen in this book, such coming together is often a first-fruit of children beginning their formal religious schooling. As the parents of such children meet one another, and the catechists and teachers of their children, in the community context of a parish, their own needs—many times unspoken and perhaps even unrealized—begin to be met in unexpected ways. The surprise of discovering friendship with other parents and the sharing of questions about our children, our church, and our God may add new and lovely dimensions to our lives. The bottom line of such surprise and sharing, however, is the mighty and ancient resource of community. As parents entering this new phase of our own and our children's lives, we need to celebrate this resource. And we need to be grateful. For whatever fosters such community is revealed as grace, and whoever fosters it is revealed as faithful.

FOR FURTHER EXPLORATION

1. *A Parish Bulletin Board:* If your parish does not have a place where notices can be displayed for those needing community assistance, bring this to the attention of the pastoral staff or parish council. Or, with your children, design one together, and give it to the parish as a gift.
2. In St. Mary's Parish, Colts Neck, New Jersey, a parish booklet is published yearly that puts together people who can serve as resources to others in the same situation. Initiated when a woman who had undergone a mastectomy suggested her name and phone number be placed in the parish bulletin, in case someone in similar circumstances might like to talk, it has grown to include references—names and numbers—of others in the community for such issues as the following: adoption, alcoholism, amputation, aging parents, child with brain damage, cardiac visitation, chronic illness, divorce, heart attack, job loss, terminal illness.

With others in your parish, or through parish staff or parish council, create a similar booklet for your community.

3. *Beyond the Parish Community:* Begin exploring the possibility of conversations between your parish community and members of another religious group in your neighborhood. Perhaps this could begin with the topics and themes raised in this book, and around the power of the faith of parents—of every tradition—in the religious education of their children.